If found
    sent
       to.
Victoria Hanratty.
7 Victoria Road
Holywood Co Down
BT18 4BA.

BODY WISE

BODY WISE
DR. PETER ROWAN

Victoria Hanratty.

London: HMSO

Devised and produced by Complete Editions

Illustrations by David Huggins
Cover Illustration by David Huggins

© Dr Peter Rowan 1993
Applications for reproduction should be made to HMSO
First published 1993

ISBN 0 11 701707 8

HMSO gratefully acknowledges the assistance given by the
Children's Hospital, Birmingham in the preparation of this book.

For Michael Hill

Contents

Introduction	1
Fit for Life	3
Your Body Type	7
Food for Sport	11
Starting to Get Fit	15
Stamina	23
Strength	31
Suppleness	35
Walking, Jogging and Running	39
Sporting Life	43
Personal Fitness Programme	47
Looking Good	49
What Makes Up Food?	55
A Healthy Diet – The Spice of Life	59
Vitamins	65
Essential Minerals	71
Appendix	
Food composition	75
Your Personal Fitness Programme	87

Introduction

Keeping your body healthy is fun. The basis of looking after it for life is to eat well, and to take a good amount of the right sort of exercise. There is a balance between food and exercises which will keep you looking and feeling good and in *Body Wise* you'll find tasty recipes and exercise tips to help you on your way.

Many sports are an opportunity not only to get fit, but to make friends. Within the book is an exercise programme that you devise to suit your needs. Maybe you want to improve your agility for dancing. Or you might want to build up your shoulder strength for canoeing. You won't need very much equipment for the *Body Wise* exercise programme, just these simple preparations:

- You must be able to count! For many of the activities you will need to time in seconds. You may have a watch that can do this. If not, then simply count aloud at a normal rate as follows, 'Body Wise One ... Body Wise Two ... Body Wise Three ...' and so on. That took about three seconds, and counting like this gives a good rough guide to time in seconds.
- Make yourself a skipping rope. You will need it for some of the exercises and tests.
- Measure out a half kilometre from your home for the running programme on page 40.

There are a couple of important points to do with food that need mentioning right away:

- The energy in food in this book is given in Calories. (1 Calorie = 1 Kcal.)
- Make sure that you don't rush into exercising straight after eating. It is never wise to exercise on a full stomach. An adequate blood supply is needed for both digestion and for exercise, and the demands of the two coming at the same time could cause one, or both activities, to suffer.

Body Wise is a positive book. You can find activities you like, and achieve your level of fitness. Within these pages is the formula for you to succeed.

CHAPTER 1

Fit for Life

A good diet and regular exercise are two key factors towards a happy, healthy and long life. The two are interlinked. Food is needed to provide the energy for exercise. It also provides the building blocks for such tissues as bone and muscle.

In its turn, exercise will make a body's muscles firm and strong, and it will also burn up dietary Calories which might otherwise turn to fat. It is also a lot of fun, and getting involved with many sports is a quick way to meet lots of new friends — of both sexes.

The symbols in this book indicate the following:

Stamina

Strength

Suppleness

What exactly is fitness?

Stamina + Strength + Suppleness = Physical Fitness.

 STAMINA: Power of endurance. Staying power (mental and physical).

 STRENGTH: Being strong. Power of resistance, not easily worn or torn, capable of exerting great muscular force.

 SUPPLENESS: Body flexibility. Pliant.

In addition to these three 'S's there is a fourth that comes with practice — SKILL.

This equation relates to physical fitness. Total body fitness incorporates all aspects of mental, social, emotional, medical, and nutritional fitness as well as physical fitness. These all fit together and interrelate like the pieces of a jigsaw.

Why bother to exercise?

Exercise will make you fit.

- You will look better.
- You will feel better.
- You are likely to live longer.

Some Food for Thought

If you are age twelve you will have eaten 5,140 kilos of food and drunk 6,857 litres of liquid. If you are age thirteen you will have eaten 5,572 kilos and drunk 7,428 litres. If you are age fourteen you will have eaten 6,000 kilos and drunk 8,000 litres

In a lifetime, the average human being living in the Western World will eat enough food to fill over 750 supermarket trolleys, and have drunk about 40,000 litres of fluids. This will weigh about 30,000 kilos — the equivalent of six African elephants.

It's obviously important to get this mixture of food right, since small daily intakes of the wrong food will add up over the years. Everything that makes up your body — except oxygen breathed in — has been taken into you through the mouth, by eating and drinking. The food *is you*. So it is important to know exactly what you are eating and drinking.

How much do you know about food? Here is an analysis of two mystery 'objects'. The figures are percentages of their total weight. Have a guess at what they are.

Object One
Water	61.50%
Protein	17.00%
Fat	14.00%
Carbohydrate	1.50%
Minerals and Vitamins	6.00%

Object Two
Water	49.00%
Protein	9.27%
Fat	13.03%
Carbohydrate	27.20%
Minerals and Vitamins	1.50%

Answer: Object One — an adult man/woman weighing 75kg

Answer: Object Two — hamburger and chips. (A 125g hamburger and a portion — 250g — of deep fried chips.)

If you didn't manage to tell hamburger and chips from a human being maybe you need to read on!

Health questionnaire – 'How health conscious are you?'

Ask yourself the following questions.

1. How often do you go to the dentist?
   a. Never.
   b. Every now and then.
   c. Every six months. ✓

2. You are in a large department store with a lift and stairs. You need to go up three floors. Would you –
   a. Wait for the lift.
   b. Use the lift if it was there. ✓
   c. Run or walk up the stairs.

3. Do you smoke?
   a. Yes.
   b. The occasional one with friends.
   c. Never. ✓

4. You are going to visit a friend who lives one kilometre away on a bus route. How would you travel?
   a. Catch the bus.
   b. Catch the bus most times.
   c. Cycle or walk. ✓

5. How often do you skip a main meal.
   a. Often.
   b. Sometimes.
   c. Never. ✓

6. About how long would it take you to walk a mile on flat ground?
   a. More than thirty minutes. ✓
   b. Between ten and twenty minutes.
   c. Less than ten minutes with some running.

7. How many times a week would you have an alcoholic drink.
   a. Most days.
   b. Perhaps once.
   c. Do not drink alcohol. ✓

8. Did you eat three fibre-rich foods yesterday? (see page 57.)
   a. No. ✓
   b. A little of one or two.
   c. Yes.

9. What would you estimate your intake of fruit and vegetables yesterday to be?
   a. Hardly any at all. ✓
   b. Less than 400 grams.
   c. More than 400 grams.

10. Consider the following and then select the most appropriate reply: Swim for twenty minutes, cycle six miles, and walk three miles.

   a. It would be very unusual for me to do any of these things.   a. ☑
   b. I have done two of these things in the last month.   b. ☐
   c. Most weeks I would do all three of these activities.   c. ☐

Your score
'a' answers score 0
'b' answers score 3
'c' answers score 5

Your result
Between:
31–50   Very health conscious.
11–30   Room for a healthier lifestyle.
0–10   Poor attitude towards your own health.

CHAPTER 2

Your Body Type

We all have different bodies and different minds, and it would be a dull world if everyone was the same. It is interesting to know what sort of body type you have, and it may help you find out which exercises or sports you are naturally suited to.

These three body types are only a guide. Most of us are somewhere between two of them, and there is a lot of overlap between these three groups.

Which body type are you?

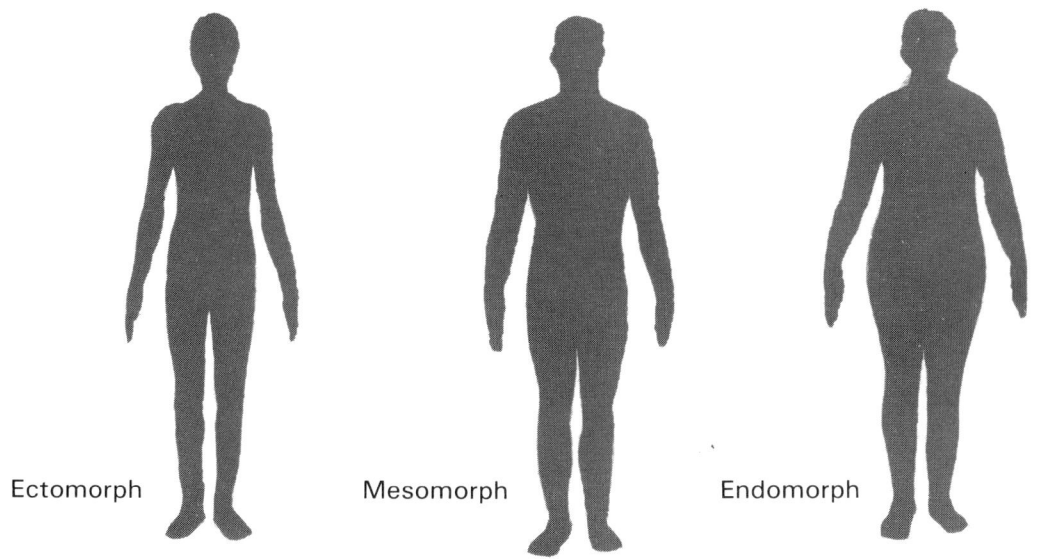

Ectomorph　　　Mesomorph　　　Endomorph

Small frame [ectomorph]

This body form has less muscle and fat than average. The hips and shoulders are narrow and from the side the silhouette is best described as 'slender'.

Medium frame [mesomorph]

The mesomorph body is often described as 'athletic'. The waist and hips are narrow compared to the shoulders which are often broad. The emphasis is on muscle and bone with little fat.

Large frame [endomorph]

Endomorphs are often described as 'chunky' and they have a heavier look than the others. The middle part of the torso tends to be on the heavy side with rounded hips wider than the shoulders.

You probably will not find an exact description of yourself here. The best way to find out if you have a natural gift for a sport or activity is to try it and see.

You can become stronger, more supple, and develop more stamina as you get fit, but you cannot change your basic body type.

Which sport for you?

Useful general guide lines to choosing a sport or activity for yourself.

Running

Sprinters tend to be muscular and thickset. Long legs and a long stride help. Muscle is heavy and it is not a disadvantage over a short explosive event like the 100 metres.

The marathon runner tends to have a much slighter body. Stamina is a great advantage, and heavy powerful muscles, which would have to be carried over the 'twenty-six mile' course, are not.

Team games

A heavy frame is an advantage in many team games, such as rugby.

Ball games

If you have a good eye for hitting a ball try cricket, hockey, squash, tennis or golf. Long arms are another advantage in a game like tennis.

You can measure your relative arm length against your own body. Put your arms against the side of your body. If your finger tips reach below mid-thigh you have long arms.

Your individual character

As well as body type you have to ask yourself what sport would suit your temperament. Do you like team games, or are you happier on your own with activities like running, cycling, or swimming?

Body tests

You'll get a good idea of your overall fitness by seeing how you perform in each of these physical tests. The nearer you get to 100 (the maximum score) the better the shape you're in.

1. Can you link your hands behind your back? Most people are right- or left-handed and tend to be more flexible on one side. You may find you can do this test one way, but not the other.
   Tests: shoulder suppleness
   Score: 7 if you can do it one way and 10 if you can do it both ways

2. Can you do the bunny hop balance while counting to ten?
   Tests: shoulder strength and overall balance
   Score: 10

3. Can you pick up a piece of A4 paper, folded lengthwise and standing upright, using your teeth and while standing on one leg as shown. Try holding each leg behind your back in turn.
   Tests: balance, legs/trunk strength, spine suppleness
   Score: 7 if you can do it on one leg, 10 if you can do it on both

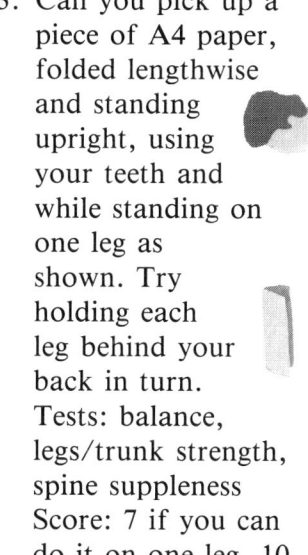

4. Can you walk along a straight twenty-metre line blindfolded?
   Tests: balance
   Score: 7

5. Can you pick up a pencil using your toes? This exercises your foot muscles. It's also an excellent exercise if you think that you might have flat feet.
   Tests: foot muscle control
   Score: 3

6. Can you balance a book on your head and walk ten metres?
   Tests: co-ordination, balance and good posture
   Score: 3

7. Can you run around a football pitch twice — running the second circuit faster than the first? (You'll need a watch to time yourself for this test.)
   Tests: stamina as well as the mental discipline to pace yourself and conserve body energy.
   Score: 10

8. Can you balance on one foot with your eyes shut for ten seconds?
   Tests: leg/hip strength and general balance
   Score: 7

9. Can you tie a knot on the floor with a ribbon using the toes of both feet?
   Tests: foot and ankle flexibility, and toe strength
   Score: 10

10. Can you throw a tennis ball in the air and then run to and from a point, five metres away, in time to catch the ball before it hits the ground?
    Tests: speed and body co-ordination
    Score: 7

11. Can you circle your left arm backwards and at the same time move the right arm forwards in the opposite circling action?
    Tests: co-ordination
    Score: 10

12. Can you put your socks on while standing on each leg in turn? No support is allowed.
    Tests: leg/hip strength and balance
    Score: 3

13. Walk on the outer edges of your feet while clapping your hands alternately up and down, first with one hand on top, then with the other.
    Tests: muscular co-ordination
    Score: 3

14. Can you take a skipping rope back over your head and down across your back as shown. Lie on your stomach with your arms in front of you, holding a piece of rope one metre long. Do not bend your arms. You will find this easier to do the further your hands are apart.
    Tests: shoulder suppleness
    Score: 7

Total Possible Score: 100

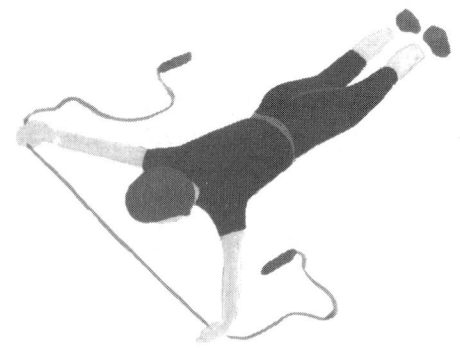

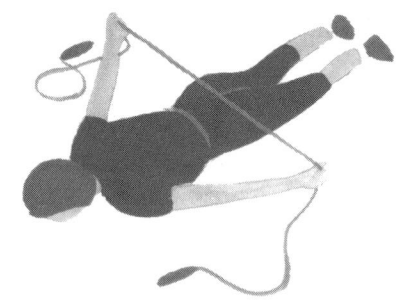

CHAPTER 3

Food for Sport

Since the body needs the energy contained in food (Calories) to run on, you would expect there to be a relationship between food and exercise. And there is. However, Calories are used not just for physical exercise, but are needed by the body for such things as: digestion, breathing and growth.

Energy

Fat, carbohydrate, protein foods and alcohol all contain energy.

- 1 gram of protein gives 4 Calories of energy
- 1 gram of carbohydrate gives 3.75 Calories of energy
- 1 gram of fat gives 9 Calories of energy
- 1 gram of alcohol gives 7 Calories of energy

The number of Calories that the body needs differs from person to person, and depends on age, sex and lifestyle.

This is the typical daily estimated average energy (Calories) needs for girls and boys of different ages — you'll see that there's a very slight variation between boys and girls.

	Estimated average daily Calorie requirement	
	Boys	Girls
Ages 11–14	2,200	1,845
Ages 15–18	2,755	2,110

There is energy contained in all food and drink except water. The amount varies a great deal from food to food. There should be a natural balance between exercise and food.

A healthy way to keep your body energy stores at the right level for *you* is to combine a balanced diet with physical exercise. Exercise burns up Calories.

Converting food to energy is called metabolism.

Exercise will raise the rate at which food is digested and burnt up (metabolic rate), and this will remain elevated if you exercise regularly.

Do not expect exercise to make you suddenly lose a lot of weight. There are two reasons why this will not happen:

- Exercise will burn up fat but develops firm and shapely muscle. However, although muscle is much more useful than fat, it is much heavier.
- It takes a lot of exercise to burn up what might appear to be a small amount of food. You need to run one kilometre to burn up the energy in four grams of butter.

If you write down *everything* you eat and drink in one day *and each food's weight*, you can use the food composition chart at the end of the book to work out your energy intake for that day. That chart analyses 100g of each food. You might like to compare this with the recommended proportions of the macronutrients – protein, fat, and carbohydrate – in the diet of an average adult. The figures are only guide lines. They do not add up to 100% since in some individuals about 5% of energy has to be allowed for alcohol intake.

Carbohydrate   50% of energy (at least)

Fat   35% of energy (maximum; ideal around 25%)

Protein   15% of energy

Cooking food

Cooking is very important in determining the nutritional value of a meal.

Consider these two basic ingredients cooked in two different ways:

White fish (cod)
Potato (100 grams)

Meal 'A'
Portion of fish deep fried in batter (325 Cals)
Deep fried potato chips (250 Cals)
Total 575 Calories

Meal 'B'
Baked cod in milk with onions, herbs and pepper cooked in a microwave (150 Cals)
Baked potato (100 Cals)

Total 250 Calories

The microwave is an excellent help in cooking if you have one to use. Food cooks very quickly, and few nutrients are lost.

The difference between these two meals of fish and potato differ greatly even though they both start with the same two basic ingredients.

Meal 'A', which is fried, is high in fat. Much goodness is lost from the original potato when it is cooked in this way.

Meal 'B', from the microwave, is a healthy meal with the protein of the fish plus the energy and fibre of the potato. Vitamins in the potato's skin have not been destroyed or lost by this method of cooking.

Food facts and fallacies

Here are half-a-dozen widely held views about food which you might like to consider. How many of these statements would you have agreed with before reading the answers?

1. Sugar is a good source of energy.
   Answer: Yes, but so are lots of foods. Sugar contains what are known as 'empty Calories'. That is they have no nutritional value other than energy (Calories). Thus they may make you fat if you do not take exercise, and may also be instrumental in depriving you of essential nutrients which are in other foods.
2. 'Starchy' foods make you put on weight.
   Answer: Not especially. Any food Calories that do not get burnt up by the body put weight on. Starchy foods such as bread and potatoes are good value. They tend to contain fibre and they have less energy (Calories) than fatty foods.
3. You need to eat red meat to get all the protein the body needs.
   Answer: No. Fish and white meat (poultry) contain the amino acids (building blocks of protein) that the body needs. Vegetarians get all their necessary protein from vegetable proteins.
4. Beer and lager are less harmful than spirits.
   Answer: This is not true. Any excess alcohol can be dangerous.
5. Brown bread is healthier than white.
   Answer: Bread is a very healthy food whatever colour. Brown bread often has more fibre, so scores points there.
6. Animal fats are high in harmful 'saturates'?
   Answer: No. There are no 'bad' fats. What is 'good' or 'bad' is how much fat, and what kind of fat is a regular part of a person's diet. Diets can be bad – not foods. And not all animal foods are high in saturates. Fish and poultry, for example, are low in 'saturates'.

CHAPTER 4

Starting to Get Fit
Stamina + STRENGTH + Suppleness = Fitness.

Not everyone finds the prospect of strenuous exercise appealing. Combine it with rules about eating foods you don't think you like, and the outlook looks even less attractive.

And if the reason given for doing all this is to avoid an unpleasant illness like a heart attack in forty years time, then the advice seems even less interesting.

'You've got to die of something' is one argument often heard against healthy living.

However, life is not all about pain and sacrifice, and this book aims to prove it. Healthy living can be about having fun, looking good, enjoying food, and making friends. You won't find a lot of 'don't do this', and 'don't do that' here.

So how fit are you?

You can get a good idea of your level of fitness by measuring your pulse rate after a set exercise test. The only equipment you will need will be a step about 20 centimetres high. The bottom step of a staircase is ideal.

How to measure your pulse rate in beats per minute

The pulse at the wrist is one of the easiest to feel. Use the finger tips of one hand to press lightly onto the inner surface of the other wrist. The area where you will feel the artery beating is about 1–2 centimetres from the wrist on the thumb side of the wrist joint.

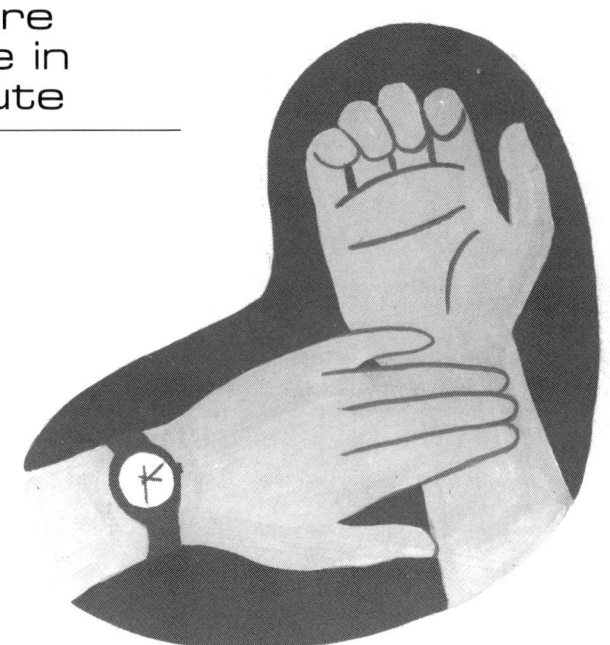

Stepping exercise test

Step up and down onto the step for 4 minutes. Step onto the step with one foot (1), and then (2) with the other foot. Put the lead foot back on the ground (3), and then return (4) the other foot to the ground.

Repeat this sequence for 4 minutes. Time this with your watch or do the stepping cycle 120 times — based on the fact that each sequence takes about 2 seconds.

After 4 minutes (or

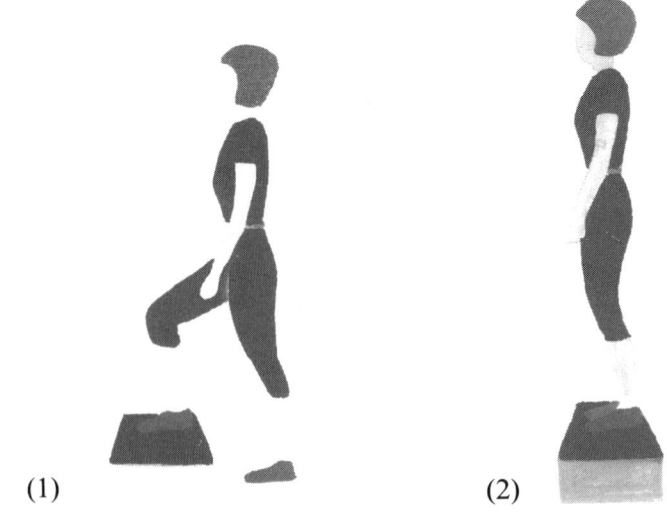

(1)   (2)

120 cycles) of this continual exercise, stop and wait exactly 30 seconds. Then count your pulse rate for the next 30 seconds. Double this figure and it will give you your heart rate in beats per minute after exercise. You can judge from the chart where you are in the fitness stakes.

Under 80 beats per minute *Very fit*
Between 80 and 95 ... ... *Fit*
Over 95 ... ... *Unfit*

 (3) 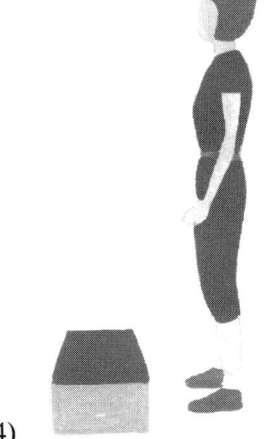 (4)

> Your pulse when you are at rest can be used to monitor improvement in fitness, since as you become fitter your resting pulse will become lower. You will use this fact to monitor the *stamina* improvement of your fitness in Chapter 5.
> Count the number of beats for 30 seconds and then double this figure. A normal heart rate at rest for teenagers is anywhere up to 75 beats per minute.

There are four different ways that you can exercise your body;

- Activities such as golf and fishing, which do not involve a great amount of exercise, but which are pleasant and relaxing.
- Exercises such as swimming, cycling and running that work the heart and circulation of the body. These are *aerobic* exercises which build stamina.
- Exercises such as weight training which build muscle *strength*.
- Stretching exercises such as yoga which build body flexibility or *suppleness*.

How to get fit – general rules

1. Make your activity fun. It doesn't have to hurt.
2. Warm up and always stretch before exercising (see page 37).
3. Exercise regularly, and build up slowly to full fitness.
4. Maintain a correct posture.
5. Avoid too much repetition of the same exercise.
6. Warm down when you have finished your activity.

If you experience any pain, faintness, or dizziness during exercise stop and get expert help.

Why bother to do warm-up exercises?

It is important to get your muscles ready for exercise. A gentle warm-up routine gets blood flowing to the muscles and stretches the joints ready for action. In the same way it is wise to 'warm down' after a burst of exercise, as this will help combat injury and stiffness in the muscles and joints.

The warm-up should increase the pulse rate to 60% of maximum. For more details of pulse rate during exercise see pages 25 & 26.

One of the best forms of warming up is skipping. Most groups of muscles are exercised, and skipping is also a very good test of co-ordination. You should not be so out of breath that you cannot speak during the exercise.

Before this warm-up you should do some stretching exercises. Remember stretching should always be static. So no bouncing into a stretch exercise. You can select your stretching exercises from those on page 37, and fit them into your personal fitness programme on page 87. If you find the idea of warming up boring then try doing the exercises to your favourite music, or a fast walk to the playing field may be just as effective as a formal routine.

Posture

What is a good posture?

Good posture is a way of standing, sitting, walking, or even sleeping in which all the various parts of the body are balanced and working together in an easy, relaxed way. This ensures that no part is put under undue strain. Good posture makes a great deal of difference to how your body looks and feels, and it says a lot about how you feel about yourself. Good posture oozes energy and confidence.

Bad posture is a tiring position to hold your body in. Its bony framework, held together and worked by ligaments, tendons and muscles, will easily tire. This can lead to strain, pain, discomfort and tension.

Lifting
Right. Protect your back by bending at the knees and lifting with a straight back.

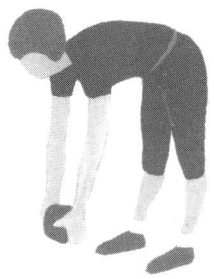

Wrong. Do not lift like this as it may damage your back.

Right   Wrong

Sitting
Right. Your back should be upright. Adjust your chair and desk so that your thighs are parallel to the ground.

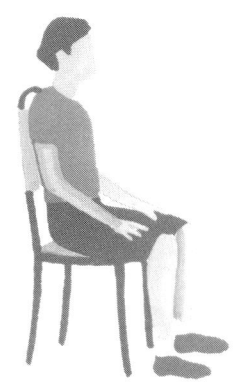

Right   Wrong

Carrying
Right. With equal weights in both hands your back and pelvis work equally on both sides.

 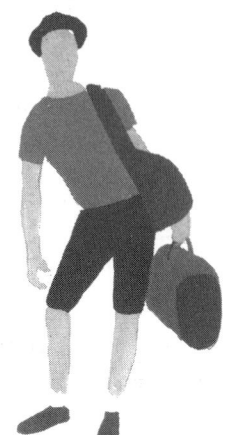

Right   Wrong

Standing
Stand up straight without slouching to one side. Your body weight should be taken equally by both legs.

Right   Wrong

Posture check

You can test your own correct standing posture in the following way:

Stand with your back to a wall. Your heels, buttocks, shoulder blades and back of head should just touch it. Fix a mirror or ask a friend to check your stance.

Most of us favour one side of the body more than the other. It is quite natural, for example, to be either right- or left-handed. However, do not ignore your 'other' side. After a game with a racket, for example, practise a few swings with this other hand and arm. This exercise helps keep an overall natural balance which will improve your game.

Good posture is the starting point of all fitness exercises.

CHAPTER 5

Stamina

STAMINA + Strength + Suppleness = Fitness.

Stamina is improved by aerobic exercises. The circulatory system – the heart and the lungs are the key parts of the body behind successful aerobics.

What exactly are aerobic exercises?

This word means exercises that use up oxygen. During aerobic exercises the pulse rate is continuously raised for twenty minutes. The heart and lungs – the 'circulatory system' – are put through their paces during this time keeping up with the extra demand for oxygen in the muscles. Regular aerobics – two to three times a week – gradually builds up stamina as well as burning off fat.

In aerobic exercise the heart and lungs work *only on available* oxygen. Thus the circulatory system is never over-stretched and is always able to supply the necessary oxygen and to take the waste products away from the muscles.

Aerobic exercises are not just the familiar routines often done to music in colourful costumes. Any sport which keeps the pulse elevated for twenty minutes is an aerobic activity and is just as beneficial.

Popular aerobic activities are: cycling, dancing, fast walking or 'power' walking, jogging, rowing, skipping, swimming.

The circulatory system

The heart is a double-barrelled pump and it works continually throughout life pumping blood around the body. The blood carries oxygen to the tissues, where it is used with 'food' to supply the body with the energy to exercise. (This energy is released as heat — which is why you get hot when you do vigorous exercise.)

When the blood returns to the heart in the veins, it is carrying waste products of exercises from the tissues. When it reaches the lungs this waste is breathed out, and more oxygen is taken in. The circulatory process then starts another cycle.

The lungs pack a huge surface area into your chest to cope with this exchange of oxygen in and waste out. It's about fifty-five square metres which, if laid out flat, is about the size of a cricket pitch (from one bowling crease to the other).

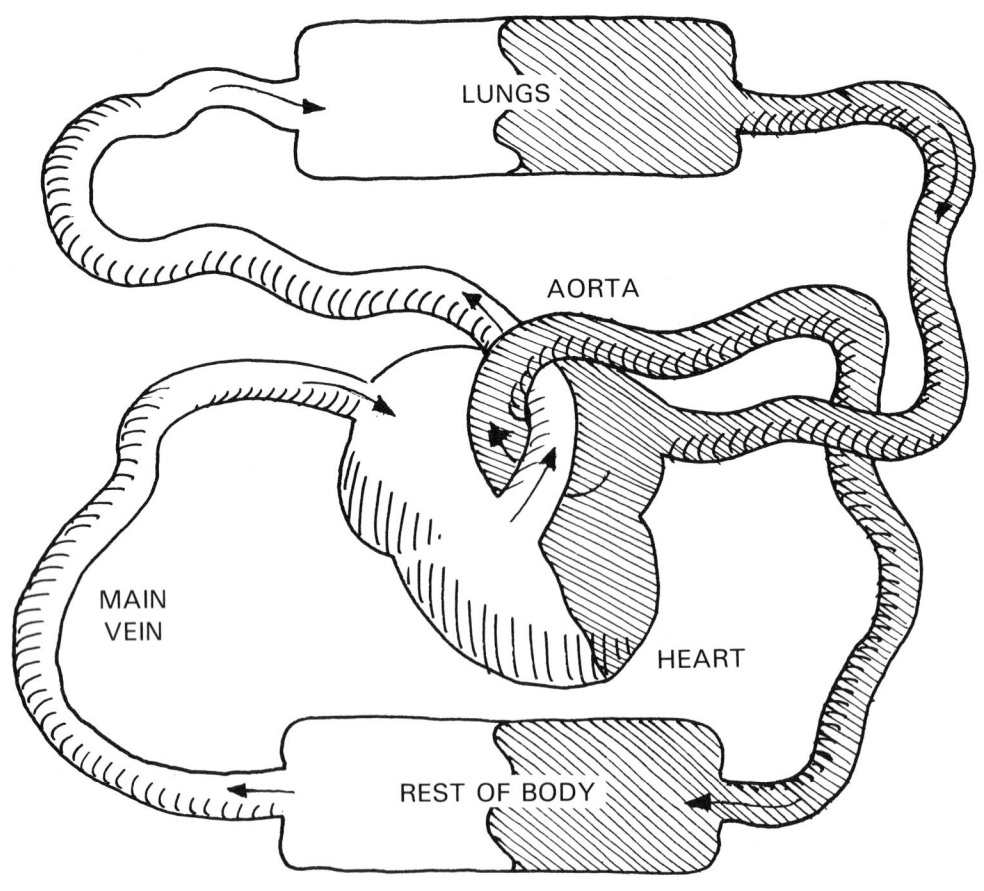

The super fit heart

The '54' factor

A fit person doing hard exercise can increase by a factor of 54 the amount of oxygen going to the muscles. This is how:
SIX times as much blood passes through the heart and lungs.
THREE times as much blood is sent to the muscles.
THREE times as much oxygen is taken from the blood by the exercising muscles.

$$6 \times 3 \times 3 = 54$$

The super fit heart develops its fitness within the 'SIX' of this '54 factor'.

With regular exercise your heart will gradually increase the amount of blood it can put out with each beat. Thus it can pump *more* blood around the body and to the muscles for the *same heart rate*.

Of course the fit heart does raise its pulse rate during exercise, but it does not have to do this nearly as much as the unfit heart. During hard exercise the fit heart may beat at 140 beats per minute. The unfit heart may need to rise to 180 beats per minute to put out the same amount of blood (see page 26 for maximum heart rate during exercise).

The *resting* heart rate of the fit athlete is actually lower than average. This is because, with the body at rest, the fit heart is quite able to pump enough blood for the body's needs at perhaps only 40 beats per minute.

Cigarette smoking can damage the lungs and slowly reduce the amount of lung available for gas (oxygen and waste) exchange. In this way it will reduce the 'SIX' factor. Cigarette smoking actually decreases the amount of oxygen carried by the blood and in this way it will adversely affect the THREE of the fitness equation.

There is only a limited amount of blood — about 6 litres — available in the circulation. As the body cannot suddenly increase this volume of blood, it must re-direct some to the muscles during exercise. This diversion comes from areas such as the skin and intestines.

If exercise is taken on a full stomach then both exercise and digestion may suffer as the blood can not be in two places at once. As blood is pulled from the intestines to the exercising muscles you may begin to feel sick.

Quick pulse measurement

Do not stop aerobics to count your pulse. You can get a fairly good measure of your pulse rate during aerobics by taking the pulse for 6 seconds then adding a nought, e.g. 10 beats in 6 seconds is a 100 beats per minute.

The pulse is the key guide to your body's response to exercise. During aerobics you should aim to keep your pulse rate between 120 and 170 beats per minute. That is between 60% and 85% of maximum heart rate.

> Doctors discovered a group of super fit Belgian cyclists had resting pulse rates of less than 30 beats per minute.

Pulse for age 15

55% – 110 beats per minute
60% – 120 beats per minute
70% – 140 beats per minute
80% – 166 beats per minute
85% – 170 beats per minute

Do not push your body above an 85% increase in heart rate (170 beats per minute). Maximum heart rate is like the top speed that a car can achieve. It's not the ideal speed for the car; it's always best to 'motor' within limits. The aim of the exercise is gradually to build your fitness up. This cannot be done quickly. As you get fitter your resting pulse will fall, as will your pulse's response to exercises.

* *

Aerobics exercises may be divided into *high* or *low impact* aerobics.

The *intensity* of aerobics can also be either *high* or *low*.

Impact refers to whether or not your feet leave the floor – and the impact that follows if they do. In aerobics *intensity* means how hard you do the exercise.

The low impact exercise of marching, for example, can be increased in intensity by picking up the knees more and using the arms.

Your aerobic exercises

As part of the aerobic section of your personal exercise plan (on page 87) you can adopt the 'Antarctic' programme below, or devise your own. The four possible types of aerobic exercises are shown below with an example of each combination of intensity and impact. But first a couple of rules to ensure the plan works and is perfectly safe:

- Mix high and low impact aerobics. Place the *high* ones in the middle of the routine. Warm up and warm down with *low* impact aerobics.
- Mix high impact/high intensity with low impact/high intensity exercises. Get the balance at about 50/50. There is a danger to the body's joints if too much high impact exercise is done.

And here is a note about what to wear on your feet:

- Running shoes are not really suitable for people who do a lot of aerobics as they tend to limit sideways movement of the foot. Many companies make 'cross trainers' which are a compromise.

Low impact
Low intensity aerobics.

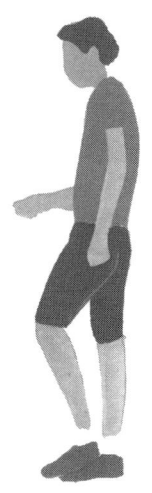

Marching on the spot.

Low impact
High intensity aerobics.

High knee pulls, alternate high knee raising by pulling down with opposite arm.

High impact
High intensity aerobics.

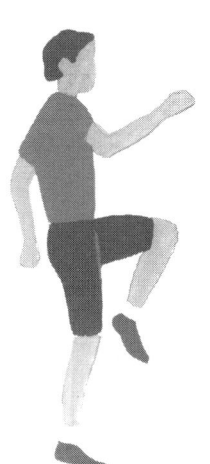

Running on the spot with knees raised to chest using arms.

High impact
Low intensity aerobics.

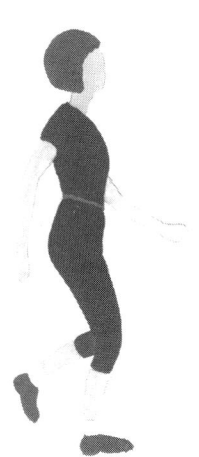

Easy jogging.

The 'Antarctic' aerobics programme

I've been on two expeditions to the Antarctic. It was important to keep fit on our ship *Discovery* and so we worked out our own exercise programme. You might like to try it and to give you an idea of how it works you'll see it filled in on the Personal Fitness Programme chart on page 48. It'll take less than thirty minutes, and I know it can be done in very limited space almost anywhere, because when we hit bad storms amongst the icebergs the captain would order us off the deck, and we simply moved down into the hold!

There is *no* resting between each routine.

All muscles to be worked in aerobics should be stretched before the exercises. You can read about these in Chapter 7, which is about being supple. For this 'Antarctic' programme the following muscle groups should be stretched using the exercises shown on pages 37 & 38. Each stretch should last about six seconds.

Stretch exercises

Calves (for skipping)	– exercise 1
Quads (for marching, sprinting and jogging)	– exercise 2
Hamstrings (for running on the spot)	– exercise 4

'Antarctic' programme

Skipping (to warm up)	4 minutes
Marching	1 minute
High knee pulls	2 minutes
Skipping	5 minutes
Jogging	2 minutes
Running on the spot	1 minute 20 seconds
Sprint at end for	10 seconds
Marching	1 minute 30 seconds
Skipping	3 minutes
Total	20 minutes

This routine lasts for twenty minutes, and you should 'warm down' (see page 18) afterwards to avoid aches and stiffness the next day. The original routine began at 3.30pm every day, and finished at 3.45pm. At the time I hadn't heard about 'aerobics' and so now I have extended it to run for the magic twenty 'aerobic' minutes. Remember the *twenty* minutes does not start until you have stretched the muscles to be used.

It also had press-ups included. I have changed these to skipping for two reasons:

- Press-ups favour boys because they are a test of shoulder strength.
- The pulse rate may fall during the press-ups, and the basis of an 'aerobics' exercise programme is to *raise the pulse rate for twenty minutes at least three times a week.*

As I've said, this programme was designed for the confined space of a ship. Once you've tried it, you create your own programme using the one on the chart on page 48 as a model.

Choose your exercises for your own personal exercise plan from these aerobics. There are many others which you can learn at aerobic classes. They all need to be learnt so that the technique is correct and will not damage or strain any part of your body. Remember, unfit people need to build up gradually to twenty minutes aerobic work. If you can speak a sentence during exercises then you are probably 'aerobic'.

Some sports are particularly good at improving stamina. You can see which in Chapter 9 on page 46.

CHAPTER 6

Strength

Stamina + STRENGTH + Suppleness = Fitness.

Body strength is the force that your muscles are able to exert. This strength can be built up by exercising the muscles. In practice exercise tends to build up a group of muscles. For example shoulder strength improves with press-ups, and the calf muscles can be strengthened by repeated standing on toes.

How you move

Muscles pull bones which then move at the joints between those bones. This is the basis of all the movements that you will do when you exercise and keep fit.

The elbow is a good one to look at to see how a joint moves.

Triceps and biceps are 'voluntary' muscles. That is they are under your direct control. You decide when to lift the weight. Involuntary muscles do work within the body which needs to happen automatically – actions such as making the heart beat, or propelling food along the digestive tract.

Strength exercises build up muscle strength by working the muscles hard for a short time. This is in contrast to aerobic exercises which work the muscles longer – twenty minutes at least – and build up stamina.

A group of muscles can be easily developed by doing light weight training. Sports centres have expensive equipment for this, but you do not need to pay money to improve your strength. Books or tins of baked beans will do just as well as dumb-bells!

Muscles need to be warmed up and stretched before exercises. This prepares them for work and with some stretching after the exercises will prevent injury and soreness. A warm-up for strength exercises is to work the muscles without weights.

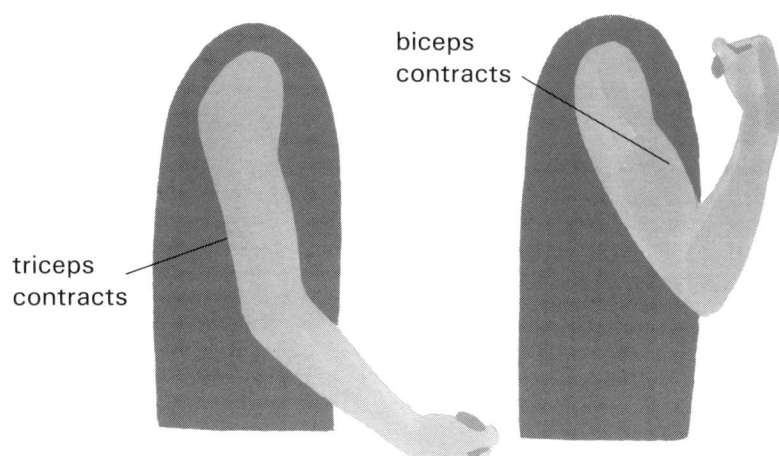

Muscles can only pull, they never push. So they tend to work in pairs. Pictured here are triceps and biceps. Biceps contracts and triceps relaxes to lift the weight.
Triceps contracts and biceps relaxes.

Eight exercises for different body muscle groups

When making up your own personal fitness programme you should aim to repeat each of these exercises until the muscle aches, and then do two more and stop.

All the exercises should be done slowly and with complete control. Remember that as well as being warmed up, muscles to be worked for increase in strength need to be stretched first. See Chapter 7 and suppleness.

1. *Abdominal.* Sit Ups. Lie flat on back with knees bent. Back should be flat on the floor at all times. With hands by ears lift up elbows towards knees.

 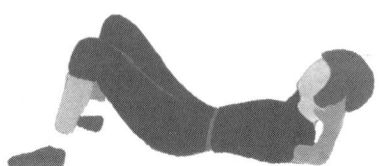

2. *Shoulder muscles.* Do half press-ups. Progress to full press-ups with staight legs and kness off the ground when you can do twenty half press-ups easily. Start with box press ups (see below) if you are not used to exercising.

3. *Biceps.* Sit on a chair holding two tins of something like baked beans. Lift these towards your chest, and then lower slowly.

4. *Triceps.* (This exercise also works biceps and pectorals — chest muscles.) Do half press-ups (see above).

If you are not familiar with press-ups then try these 'box' press-ups first.

Important points. Tilt the pelvis to keep a straight back. Do not 'snap' back elbows. Keep weight forward over arms.

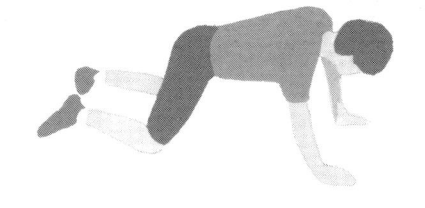

5. *Buttocks.* Lie flat on the floor with your hands by your side. Raise each leg in turn as high as you can. Keep the leg straight and point your toes. Hold this position for a count of five then slowly lower your legs. This exercise will get your behind in good shape. The hips must stay on the floor.

6. *Thighs.* (Quadriceps or 'quads'.) Sit on a chair and fully straighten the knee. Do both legs together.

8. *Hamstrings.* (The muscles at the back of the thigh.) Get into 'box' press ups position, and then straighten one leg out so that it's level with body. Then bring heel to buttock and repeat.

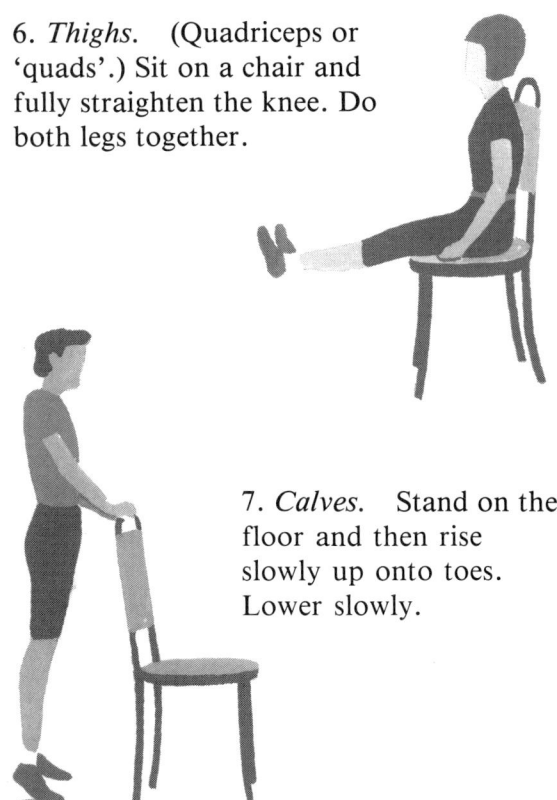

7. *Calves.* Stand on the floor and then rise slowly up onto toes. Lower slowly.

Some sports are particularly good at improving muscle strength. You can see this in Chapter 9. Canoeing, for example, strengthens the muscles of the arms, shoulders and upper back.

Rowing strengthens the legs and the lower back as well as the arms. Most of the power that propels the boat through the water comes from the legs.

CHAPTER 7

Suppleness

Stamina + Strength + SUPPLENESS = Fitness.

Suppleness means having a flexible and pliant body, which can stretch and bend with ease. The human body is not a rigid structure — even bones bend — but most of the flexibility that comes with fitness originates from the muscles, joints and ligaments associated with the bones.

Joints

There are basically two sorts of joints between bones: fixed joints and mobile joints.

Fixed joints

Tough fibrous bones exist between the bones of the skull. They are strong and hardly move at all.

Mobile joints

The joints most involved in fitness exercises are the large mobile joints such as the wrist, elbow, hip, knee and ankle. There are many other smaller joints, like those between the bones of the fingers and toes, involved in movement too.

The joints of the body vary in their range of movement, and they are designed according to how they are expected to operate in real life.

Thus the shoulder is one of the most mobile. It has a huge range of movement to enable the arm to move.

The knee is much less mobile. However, it makes up for this by being just about the strongest joint the body has. It needs to be, because it is one of the primary weight bearing joints of the body.

You can test your shoulder suppleness by trying 'Can you' number 1 on page 9 and number 14 on page 10.

Ligaments

These are tough fibrous cords between two bones at a joint. These are flexible, but they will not stretch. They set the limits beyond which a joint is unable to move. Without ligaments joints would easily come out of joint (dislocate.)

If a joint is moved beyond its normal range of movement the ligaments may tear. These injuries are called sprains, and may take a while to heal because the fibrous tissue of ligaments mends slowly.

Tendons

These fibrous cords tether muscles to bone. They are very, very strong and if you pull one violently it will usually pull a piece of bone away rather than break itself.

Cartilage

This tissue is a tough, smooth white gristle which cushions and protects the ends of the bones. Synovial fluid lubricates the joint.

Benefits of being supple and having a flexible body

- Your movements will be smooth, graceful and well co-ordinated.
- Keeping your body supple reduces the risk of injury and stiffness after exercise.

Ballet dancers are some of the most supple athletes. They are able to move gracefully into different positions, while always keeping a good posture. Exercises for ballet concentrate on being able to twist, bend and stretch with ease.

To test your general body suppleness try 'Can you' Test 13 on page 10.

Suppleness exercises for fitness programme

Suppleness is achieved by stretching exercises. Each of the following are designed to stretch a specific muscle group. It is vital to warm up and then to stretch muscles before exercising them. Hold each position for ten seconds. *Do not bounce* into a stretch exercise.

1. *Calf.* Front leg bent with knee over heel. Back leg straight. Toes point forward.

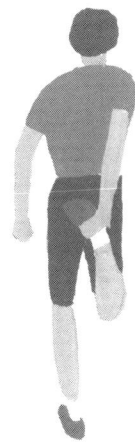

2. *Quads.* Bend supporting leg. Hold ankle. Knees together.

3. *Hip Flexors.* (These muscles move the hip.) Knee over heel (you should be able to lift up the toes of front foot). Hands either side of front foot. Drop hip towards floor.

7. *Triceps.* Hand between shoulder blades. Overpressure with other arm. Head and shoulders relaxed. Knees bent. Pelvis tilted.

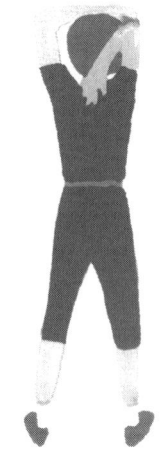

4. *Hamstrings.* Ease weight forward. (You may not be able to reach as far as in diagram.) Head and shoulders up.

8. *Pectorals.* Hands behind back. Squeeze shoulder blades together.

5. *Adductors.* (Leg adductors move the leg towards the body.) Sit up and lean forward. Gentle pressure on knees with elbows.

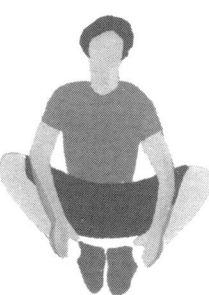

6. *Lower Body.* (Gluteus maximus and hamstrings.) Thigh to chest. (Hold under knee.) Straighten lower leg. Hips stay on floor. Head and shoulders relaxed.

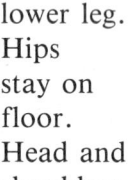

Stretching exercises should produce an easily felt tension in the muscle(s) being stretched. There should be no pain or shaking — this indicates that you have gone too far.

Some sports are particularly good at improving body suppleness. You can see which in Chapter 9.

CHAPTER 8

Walking, Jogging and Running

Walking, jogging and running are at the heart of most activity sports.

Walking

Walking is an excellent form of fitness training, and exercises the muscles of the legs as well as the heart and lungs. Walking uses over half of the body's 600-plus muscles, and will gradually build up your body's level of fitness. If you can vary the terrain you will exercise even more muscle groups.

Jogging

Jogging is an exercise between running and walking. You should be able to speak while out for a jog. If you can't you are overdoing the exercise.

Running

Running is for the fully fit. Build up to this vigorous exercise through walking and jogging. Many athletics clubs give support and competition for the keen runner.

This programme is designed to take your body from a fairly poor state of fitness to a state where you will be able to run for twenty minutes while maintaining a pulse rate between 130–160 beats per minute.

Running for four miles (6.4 km) is equivalent to swimming for one mile (1.6 km) or cycling for ten miles (16 km). Each of these uses the same amount of energy as one hour of high impact aerobics.

Good running shoes are vital. You'll save yourself a lot of trouble if you choose carefully, and be prepared to spend a little more money to get the best quality.

Look for:

- Thick pliable soles – to cushion your feet.
- Leather – to avoid the excess heat that plastic will retain.
- Good ankle support – to avoid twisting the joint.
- A good fit – for comfort and to avoid blisters. When you put the shoe on there should be one centimetre between your big toe and the end of the shoe. Often you need a half size bigger than your normal shoe size.
- Short laces – long laces just get in the way and may trip you up.

Tip to avoid blisters – wear two pairs of socks. A thin cotton pair next to the skin, and a thicker outer pair to rub against the shoe.

A personal twelve-week training programme for jogging

There are all sorts of running plans which build up fitness. For the first six weeks this one keeps the time spent exercising at twenty minutes and gradually increases the amount of running.

In the second six weeks of the programme the distance stays constant and you will be racing against yourself.

One tip is to run away from home for half the time, and run back in the second half of the programme. That way you always finish at home. Try to walk and run 'home' slightly faster than on the 'out' section. This ensures that you warm up well before running fast.

Each week this regime is done three times.

Week One	Walk	20	minutes
Week Two	Walk	16	minutes
	Run	4	minutes
Week Three	Walk	10	minutes
	Run	10	minutes
Week Four	Walk	4	minutes
	Run	16	minutes
Week Five	Walk	2	minutes
	Run	18	minutes
Week Six	Run	20	minutes.

At the end of week six you should mark the furthest point travelled. If you are running away from home and then back, this will be the distance run in ten minutes.

In weeks seven to ten you run against *time*. Try and travel to the point reached in week six in a faster time each week. Remember you are competing against yourself. Build up speed each week, otherwise it will be very difficult to better your time each week. (Fill in your own time below.)

Week seven   Time taken: ....

Week eight   Time taken: ....

Week nine   Time taken: ....

Week ten   Time taken: ....

Week eleven   Time taken: ....

Week twelve   Time taken: ....

Running tips – how to avoid problems and injuries

- Use good footwear. See above. Trim toe nails.
- Try and run on various surfaces, and on different terrain. Going up hills will exercise your muscles in different ways. Avoid hard surfaces for the first few weeks.
- Build up with a good training programme as above.
- Run in your own natural way. Allow the heel to hit the ground first – not the toes – and you will quickly fall into your own easy and relaxed style.
- Pay special attention to warming up exercises; in addition 'warm down' after to avoid stiffness. The stretch exercises involved are very important for your body.
- Warm weather jogging – Maintain a good fluid intake during your longer runs.
- Cold weather jogging – Keep warm – particularly the upper body which should be well clothed. Gloves are necessary in very cold weather.

CHAPTER 9

Sporting Life

Sport should be fun. There isn't a 'fun' entry in the chart on page 46 because what is fun to one person may not be to another. Roller-skating, for example, would get a high 'fun' rating in most people's chart, but not in everyone's.

A lot of people find it hard to stay fit because they pick activities that they do not really enjoy.

Clothes for sport

I've already mentioned the importance of wearing the right footwear for aerobics and running and wearing the right clothes also makes a difference, whatever sport you do.

As a general rule choose loose cotton clothes that give freedom of movement; these allow sweat to evaporate, while keeping the body warm. It is important to keep muscles warm as you exercise them. Wear layers of loose fitting clothes that you can peel off as you warm up. A tracksuit is very useful to wear when you warm up and warm down.

For cycling, wear cotton T-shirt and shorts in the summer, and warm loose fitting clothes such as a track suit in colder weather. A waterproof jacket is essential in wet weather.

Wear some sort of protective head gear as motorcyclists have to by law. Special aerodynamic, light-weight helmets are now available for cyclists. Brightly coloured clothing is ideal. You look good and you can be seen by motorists.

Some sports such as squash and skiing carry a small risk to the eye. Glasses are available to protect the eye from a squash ball, and to shield the eye of the skier from bright sunlight reflected off snow in the mountains. Play safe with your eyes if there is even any remote danger, and wear a pair of the very trendy sports glasses that are available.

Serious swimmers prefer one piece swimming costumes. Leave bikinis for beach posers. Goggles will protect your eyes if you find chlorine in the water irritating.

Popular sports

Cycling

This is a brilliant form of exercise which strengthens and shapes the legs, as well as keeping the heart and lungs in good working order. Of all exercises cycling is one of the easiest to build into the routine of your life. Thus a method of transport becomes a pleasant way to keep in shape.

Swimming

Many athletes, of whatever sport, feel that swimming is the best form of exercise. It is certainly an excellent exercise for the heart (circulation) and lungs (breathing). It uses most muscle groups of the body, and of course it is a non-weight bearing exercise. This means, amongst other things, that it is perfect for the bones and joints of the spine, as well as all weight bearing joints. When swimming your backbone is horizontal and not in a weight bearing or supportive position. This keeps the spine supple and flexible.

In addition to all this the swimmer is always exercising against resistance — the water. Even the best designed weight training programmes, or the most expensive exercise machines do not achieve this. All you need is water!

As well as being an aerobic exercise, if you can master the four basic strokes, swimming has the increased benefit of using different muscle groups in different ways. This puts the joints through different sets of movements.

The *crawl* is a good all-round exercise, especially for breathing and co-ordination.

The *breast stroke* is a good exercise for the muscles of the arms, chest and legs.

The *back stroke* is a more leisurely stroke.

The *butterfly* is a very good aerobic exercise which uses up a lot of energy.

Badminton

A fast game which can be played indoors or out, and long rallies call for a great deal of concentration.

Dancing

A form of exercise which burns up a variable amount of Calories. It depends how vigorously you dance!

Pop mobility

Exercises done to music are ideal since they make the work involved more fun. Specific aerobic shoes are available which allow the foot to move sideways as well as up and down.

Tennis

Played hard it builds up the legs and arms as well as giving the heart and lungs a good work out. As with any sport it is worth taking lessons at an early stage if you have any ambition to compete at a high level. If not, just have fun and exercise at the same time as meeting people and making friends.

Canoeing

This sport builds up muscular strength of the arms and shoulders in particular.

Squash

Of all the ball and racket games squash probably requires the most stamina.

Riding

Horse riding develops the muscles of the back, bottom and legs.

Fitness factors

The chart on the next page gives some ideas of how various sports can develop your stamina, strength and suppleness — the components of physical fitness.

	Stamina	Strength	Suppleness
Aerobics	5	2	4
Badminton	2	1	2
Basketball	3	2	2
Canoeing	3	3	2
Climbing stairs	3	2	1
Cricket	1	1	2
Dancing (disco)	3	2	4
Fishing (coarse)	1	1	1
Fly fishing	1	1	2
Golf	1	1	3
Handball	3	2	3
Field Hockey	3	2	2
Martial arts	3	3	3
Netball	3	2	3
Pop mobility	3	2	3
Horse riding	1	2	1
Rowing	4	4	2
Rugby (forward play)	3	4	1
Rugby (running backs)	3	2	2
Running	3	3	2
Sailing (dinghies)	1	2	2
Skating (ice)	3	2	3
Skating (roller)	2	2	3
Skiing (cross country)	5	3	3
Skiing (downhill)	2	3	3
Skiing (water)	2	3	2
Skipping	3	1	2
Football (soccer)	2	3	2
Speed skating	4	4	2
Squash	4	2	4
Tennis	2	2	3
Volleyball	4	2	4
Walking briskly	2	1	1
Weight training	1	4	2
Windsurfing	2	3	3

CHAPTER 10

Personal Fitness Programme

Keeping fit and looking in good shape is a very personal pastime. So in this part of the book *you* decide what you wish to achieve with an exercise programme, and then work one out for yourself.

Before we work a programme out together for you there are three important things to remember:

First *always* warm up before your programme.

Second *always* stretch different muscle groups before exercising.

Third *always* warm down after an exercise routine.

The programme is in four parts:

- Stretch exercises
- A warm-up aerobic exercise – skipping.
- Main section – alternates between aerobics and muscle conditioning (strength) exercises.
- A warm-down aerobic exercise – skipping.

As I've already mentioned, aerobics can range from running to swimming. There is a wide range of activities which can be called aerobics. Some need expensive equipment like exercise bikes, but many don't.

For our programme only simple ones which can be done easily and anywhere – from the Antarctic to a high-rise flat – are included. The *main section* is what is sometimes called aerobocircuits. That is a mixture of aerobics and circuit training.

Strength + Stamina + Suppleness = FITNESS

Suppleness (stretch exercises)	Time: Minutes	Warm-up	Stamina/strength exercises	Warm-down
Calf stretch (exercise 1) Quads stretch (exercise 2) Hamstrings stretch (exercise 4) 6 seconds each				
Antarctic Programme	1	⎫		
	2	⎬ Skipping		
	3	⎪		
	4	⎭		
	5		⎫ Marching	
	6		⎬	
	7		⎭ High knee pulls	
	8			
	9			
	10		⎫ Skipping	
	11		⎭	
	12			
	13		⎫ Jogging	
	14		⎭	
	15		Running on the spot with 10 second sprint at the end	
	16			
	17		Marching	
	18			⎫
	19			⎬ Skipping
	20			⎭

You will find a blank Personal Fitness Programme chart for your own use on page 87.

CHAPTER 11

Looking Good

Hair

Healthy hair is a vital part of looking and feeling good. Each hair grows out from a growing point called a follicle. There are thousands all over the body, but the greatest collection is on the top of the head.

There are between 100,000 and 150,000 hairs growing out of the top of your head at the moment. Each person naturally sheds about 100 hairs a day.

Hair colour, texture, and waviness are part of your genetic code. It is possible to change this temporarily of course, with such things as dyes and perms.

Types of hair

Blonds tend to have the greatest number of hairs, but each one tends to be very fine.

Red-heads tend to have the fewest numbers of hairs, but each individual hair is coarser than blond hair.

Straight hair grows out from a round follicle. Wavy hair grows out from an oval follicle. Curly hair grows out from a flat follicle.

Straight　　　　Wavy　　　　Curly

Dry or greasy?

Teenage hair is almost always greasy because teenage hormones stimulate oil glands around the hair follicle on the scalp. Try this test to see if your hair is dry or greasy:

- Wash your hair with your normal shampoo.

- Leave it two days then look carefully at it. If it is 'light' and blows out of control easily it is 'dry'.

  On the other hand it may look greasy, and be stuck to your scalp in strands.

Shampooing hair

Wash your hair when it looks as if it needs it. There are no rules about how often this should be done. Use only enough shampoo to get a good lather, massage the scalp gently, and then rinse the shampoo off after a few minutes. Shampoo only needs to be in contact with hair for less than a minute to cleanse it.

The occasional use of a conditioner will make it easier to comb, gives it a shine, and will give some protection against the heat of a hair dryer.

Hair dryers – especially used hot – may damage the hair and dry out the scalp. Do not set them at maximum heat, and hold them at least 15 centimetres from the scalp. Keep the air stream moving as you blow dry.

Myths about hair care

- 'Wearing a hat causes baldness'. Untrue. Baldness – the so-called male pattern baldness – which comes to many males is decided by the genetic programme present at birth. Nothing can be done about this.
- 'Cutting hair makes it grow faster'. Untrue. If you wish to grow your hair do not have it cut.
- 'Washing hair makes it fall out'. Untrue. Hairs are falling out – and being replaced by new growth – all the time. You will notice this, of course, when you wash your hair.
- 'Dandruff is catching'. Untrue.
- 'Split ends can be repaired'. Untrue. The only treatment is to cut them off.

Common hair problems

Dandruff
Dandruff is a build up of dry dead skin on the scalp. (The cells of the scalp are naturally being shed continually.)

If this becomes excessive and bothers you, buy a shampoo with selenium in it. This will soften the surface of the scalp and help prevent dandruff.

Split Ends
A common problem in which hair – usually dry hair – splits at the end. Trim hair ends to prevent splits extending up the hair. The problem can be prevented by looking after your hair and using a conditioner if it becomes dry.

Most teenage hair problems such as flaky scalp and split ends are caused by giving the hair and the scalp a hard time with the hair drier, heated rollers, bleaches, colouring, and other such harsh treatments. A healthy head of hair comes naturally with body fitness and a good diet.

Feet

Foot care

Apart from the occasional toe nail cutting, feet are often a forgotten part of the body. However, it's worth taking care of them to avoid problems such as ingrowing toe nails, bunions (deformity at the base of the big toe), and corns (hard thick dead skin from the pressure of badly fitting shoes).

- Wear shoes that fit and are comfortable. Poor footwear accounts for most foot problems.
- Go barefoot as often as possible.
- Wash feet daily and dry between toes.
- Avoid wearing the same shoes every day, and put on clean socks each morning.
- Exercise is good for the feet (see 'Can You' Question 5 on page 9).

Nails

Nails are a hard extension of the skin. They grow out from the nail bed at the base of the nail. In teenagers they grow faster than at any other time of life. In one month finger nails grow about 2 millimetres. The middle nail grows the fastest of all.

Good nail care

- Shape to an oval at the end of a finger nail. Filing is better than clipping with a metal nail clipper since this may cause the nail to split.
- Keep your nails reasonably short. They are easier to look after and will not interfere with sports.
- If your nails tend to split, clear nail varnish will give the nail additional strength.
- Cut or file across toe nails. This will prevent the edge of the nail cutting into the flesh at the side of nail – an ingrowing toe nail. This painful condition is most common in the big toe.

Hearing

Take care of your hearing

Your ears are well worth looking after. Deafness in later life can be a terrible handicap, and could often have been prevented by taking better care of hearing.

Exposure to loud noise over a period of time damages the delicate inner workings of the ear. At first hearing loss is temporary, but it soon becomes permanent if noise exposure continues.

A good guide to noise level estimation is that if sound makes normal conversation difficult, then the noise level could be damaging your hearing.

Sound is measured in decibels:

Decibels
- 10 softest sound humans can hear.
- 20 a whisper.
- 60 talking normally.
- 80 heavy traffic.
- 90 loud shout.
- 100 rock concert.
- 110 disco.
- 115 road drill.
- 120 world record for screaming.
- 130 jet aircraft taking off.
- 140 gun shot.

Wax in the ear is a natural substance produced to lubricate and protect the lining of the ear canal. The lining cells of this canal produce small amounts continually. Excess wax can obviously reduce hearing.

The best way to avoid this is to avoid poking things down the ears. Cotton buds, finger tips, and corners of towels may simply push the wax down towards the ear drum, and cause it to build up.

Skin

Skin and the sun

Many sports, exercises, and fun games take place in the sun. Most of us love to feel the warmth of the sun on our backs; but without some care sun, and its ultraviolet rays, can cause skin problems.

The ultraviolet rays in the sun can cause premature ageing of the skin, and can make rare forms of skin cancer more likely to develop.

Sun Rules
- Avoid getting sunburnt.
- Tan slowly.
- Remember: SLIP, SLOP, SLAP – SLIP on a shirt, SLOP on sun cream, and SLAP on a hat.

There are a wide variety of skin care products available for the sun. Most of them are marked with factor numbers. In general the higher the factor the more UV light is filtered out. Beware of swimming and washing the creams and lotions off. Many are marked 'water resistant' but need to be re-applied after a swim. All of us need to be especially careful in the first few days of exposure to the sun.

The right protection for your skin

Skin type		Skin protection factors		
		Moderate sun UK. Northern Europe	Hot Mediterranean	Very hot Tropics
Fair	burns very very easily and never tans (fair or no hair, pale skin and freckles)	10–15	15	15+
Light	burns easily (blue eyes and fair hair)	4–8	6–10	8–15
Medium	burns on prolonged exposure (dark hair and eyes)	2–6	4–8	6–10
Dark	rarely burns (dark hair and eyes, black or olive skin)	2	2–4	4–6

Teeth

Teeth need cleaning. It may be boring, but it will save a lot of pain, discomfort and trouble later on. They should last you a lifetime. Healthy looking teeth are part of one of the most attractive actions – smiling. Rotten or dirty teeth are a turn-off.

Plaque – what is it and how to avoid it

Plaque is a mixture of food, saliva and bacteria. You can't see it, but it builds up between teeth and along the gum line and within a short period of time the bacteria produce acid which attacks the teeth – eventually leading to holes in them. After a while the plaque hardens to what is called tartar or calculus. This can only be removed by dental instruments. This process is called scaling. On regular visits to the dentists, say twice a year, this deposit can be removed.

Tooth and gum disease is the most common health problem in the world – yet it is quite easily prevented.

Rules for healthy teeth

- Cut down on sugar and sweet foods and drinks.
- Go to the dentist regularly – say twice a year.
- Clean your teeth morning and night.
- Replace your tooth brush when the bristles get bent and worn.

Braces for teeth

No-one would choose to have a mouth full of metal unless it was necessary, but crooked teeth are easy to move around between the ages of about twelve to sixteen, and metal braces will do this. They are fitted by the dentist, and will need to be in place for perhaps a year.

CHAPTER 12

What Makes Up Food?

Eating food may sometimes seem a complicated business, but there are really only three things to be done with a meal. This is why we all need to eat:

- For growth and any necessary body repairs.
- For energy.
- To stay healthy. Many key elements in foods are present in minute quantities, yet they are vital for life. The vitamins are an excellent example.

The components of food and what makes up the human body are analysed on page 4.

These are:

Protein
Fats
Carbohydrates – including fibre } macronutrients

Vitamins and minerals } micronutrients

Water

Protein

Protein is essential for growth, and for all the necessary day to day repair and replacement that is always taking place in the body. Skin cells, for example, are being rubbed off all the time and new ones formed. Young people who are growing obviously need a greater proportion of protein than adults.

Proteins are made up of amino acids. These are linked together in different combinations to make the different proteins. The amino acids are like the letters of the alphabet. When joined together these amino acids, or 'letters', form proteins. Proteins are the equivalent of words.

There are over twenty different types of amino acids in your body. Most can be made by the body, however eight can not be, and they must be taken in as food.

Food sources of protein are: meat, fish, nuts, beans, peas, grains, milk and cheese.

Fats

Fat is used by the body to give energy. In 1866 two scientists measured the amount of fat in a dead pig. They found that there was more fat in the carcase than the pig had been given to eat during its entire life. It was clear from this experiment that the additional fat must have been converted into fat from something else — carbohydrates in fact.

The two reasons the body does this are:

- Fat is a very efficient way to store energy. Weight for weight fat has more energy (Calories) than other foods. A piece of fat produces twice the amount of energy as the same weight of carbohydrate (see page 11).
- Once stored, the fat can be kept for leaner times. This was more important when our ancestors couldn't rely on being able to go to the supermarket or fridge whenever they felt hungry.

People get 'fat' when fat builds up in the body's stores, instead of being used up to provide energy. To scientists, fat may be molecules of carbon, oxygen and hydrogen, but to the over-weight fat is seen as a 'spare tyre' around the midriff.

Apart from being an energy food, fats are essential for building body cell walls, and for making certain hormones. In addition some fats contain vitamins A and D. Fat is also a good 'blanket' against cold when it is stored under the skin.

Foods with a more than 30% fat content include: butter, margarine, chocolate, hard cheeses, and salted peanuts.

Foods with *no* fat include: sugar, egg white, and most drinks which do not contain milk.

Carbohydrates

There are three types of carbohydrate: simple sugars, starches and cellulose.

Simple sugars

These carbohydrates, such as glucose, maltose and fructose, are found naturally in milk and fruits. Sugar is also added to foods such as sweets, cakes and ice cream, and it is often added to sweeten drinks such as tea and coffee.

Starches

Starches are the energy stores of plants. The potato is a good example of a starchy food. In a healthy diet starches are more important than the simple sugars because the foods which contain them have fibre.

Foods with both starch and fibre are often said to be wholefoods or unrefined. This combination of starch and fibre is found in: potatoes, whole grain rice, wholemeal bread and wholewheat pasta.

Cellulose

This form of carbohydrate is better known as roughage or fibre. Fibre gives plants their shape. It forms the 'bones' of the plants.

Fibre is a very important part of food even though it has no nutritional value, is not absorbed by the body, and goes straight through you and down the toilet. The reason for this is that fibre adds bulk to food, and gives your intestines something to 'grip' onto. You can avoid constipation and many other bowel problems by eating plenty of fibre as part of your diet. High-fibre foods are satisfying as they give a feeling of being full without making you fat. You can eat as much fibre as you like without putting weight on, as the body cannot convert it into energy (Calories).

The healthy effects of fibre are not confined to the bowel. It may also have a beneficial effect on the blood levels of sugar and cholesterol; this may have good long-term effects on the heart and circulation.

High-fibre foods include: whole grain breads, cereals, fruits, peas, beans and brown rice. (There is no fibre in food of animal origin.)

Floater or sinker – Which are you?
Have a look next time you have your bowels open. 'Floaters' are produced by people who eat plenty of fibre. Fibre makes for soft bulky stools. 'Sinkers' come from the bowels of those who do not eat enough fibre. The stools are small, hard and they sink.

Many people get much of their daily fibre from eating potatoes. Although potatoes are not particularly high in fibre, the fact that they are eaten regularly makes them a significant fibre source for a lot of us.

Vitamins and minerals

Thirteen vitamins and nine minerals are now known to be needed by the human body to keep it healthy. These may only be needed in minute quantities, but they are very important parts of our diet, so there's a whole chapter about each of them starting on page 65.

Alcohol

Alcohol (ethyl alcohol) is formed in nature by the fermentation of sugar. Man uses it for a number of purposes:

- As a disinfectant
- As a drug
- For food
- As a preservative

Alcohol contains energy (Calories) and has no other nutritional value. Unlike the other nutrients mentioned in this chapter it is not essential to the body.

Many people use alcohol quite harmlessly to relieve stress and overcome shyness in social gatherings. Moderate social drinking does not harm health, and may have some benefits to well-being.

However, there are hazards associated with it, and sadly for some people alcohol becomes a dangerous drug and a threat to health. They may start binge drinking, or become accustomed to a heavy regular intake.

Alcohol consumption is measured in units. One unit equals:

1 small glass wine
$\frac{1}{2}$ pint average strength beer or lager
$\frac{1}{3}$ pint strong export beer or lager
$\frac{1}{6}$ pint barley wine
1 pub measure of spirits
1 glass sherry
$1\frac{1}{2}$ pints low alcohol beer

All the above contain 8 grams of alcohol. From this and the equation below it is easy to work out how many Calories a day a person can obtain from alcohol with its high energy content but zero nutritional rating.

1 pint of beer = 2 units = 16 grams alcohol = 112 Calories = 10 minutes skipping

CHAPTER 13

A Healthy Diet – The Spice of Life

We are lucky in the Western World to have an abundance of food types and this should make eating a good healthy enjoyable diet easy. Food is important to all of us – and variety is literally the spice of life.

A healthy diet takes the necessary daily vitamins, minerals and protein, and is careful with fats and sugars.

There is no such thing as 'junk' food, only junk diets. If you eat a well-balanced diet of a mixed variety of foods you are well on the way to healthy eating.

Basis of a healthy diet

- What the food is.
- What happens to food before you get it.
- How food is cooked.
- The balance between all the different foods in a meal.
- How much food you eat.

What the food is

Western diets tend to be high in fats. Fats have a lot of Calories in them and excess will result in obesity. Fats can easily creep into your diet without you realizing. Pastry, sausages and crisps all contain significant amounts of fat.

There are two types of fat in food. They are known as saturated and unsaturated fats. Most foods contain both. Eating too much fat can cause narrowing of the blood vessels, as fatty substances are laid down in the walls of arteries. For a healthy heart and circulation it is important to eat less fat, and in particular to change to foods with less saturated fat.

Saturated fats – ('saturates') are found in meat fats and dairy products, such as butter. They can also be 'hidden' in biscuits, cakes, puddings and chocolate.

Unsaturated fats – ('unsaturates') are found in vegetable oils such as sunflower and olive oils, in nuts, and in oily fish like herring, trout, sardines, mackerel and pilchards.

Sugar can be another dietary enemy. It contains Calories (energy) but very little else in the way of nutrients. Thus it contributes to obesity, as well as rotting teeth.

Many foods have sugar 'hidden' in them. Canned or bottled soft drinks, sweets, cakes, ketchup all contain significant amounts of 'hidden' sugars.

What happens to food before you get it

We all eat frozen or canned food at sometime or other. These methods of preserving food either slow down, or stop microbes 'making the food bad'. Also packaging protects food from contamination. However, when food is heated prior to canning some nutrients are lost. To a lesser extent the same happens when food is frozen.

Most packaged foods have salt added to give flavour. Excess salt over a long period of time may be harmful to the body.

How food is cooked

The way that many foods are cooked affects their value to the body when they're eaten. Overcooking vegetables destroys or removes many of the nutrients.

Salt is very often added to food in cooking or when it arrives on the table, and, as I've said, most packaged foods have salt added to them. The result of this is that many people eat three to four times more salt than they need, and this places them at risk from developing high blood pressure.

The balance between all the different foods in a meal

Your diet needs to have balance. If you eat a high fat diet you get all your calories from the fat, and so tend to eat less carbohydrates. Carbohydrates contain healthy fibre. Food processing in factories can often remove natural fibre from food.

How much food you eat

Many people simply overeat. There is a temptation to eat too much fat since fat stays around in the stomach longer than other foods, and gives a pleasant 'full' feeling.

Try these *positive* eating habits:

- Eat white meat, low fat cheese and fish. Replace butter with margarine.
- Drink semi-skimmed milk.
- For snacks eat fruit and fresh vegetables rather than sugary snacks.
- Drink natural fruit juices rather than too much tea and coffee.
- Eat fresh food wherever possible.
- Grill, poach, or bake food rather than fry it. Use herbs and spices rather than salt to give flavour. Do not overcook. Boiling food washes out more nutrients than steaming.
- Eat lots of different kinds of food.
- Increase your fibre intake.
- Eat slowly until you are comfortably 'full'. If you carry on after this you may well get fat.

Diets

On page 7 you can see the basic body type that you were born with. There is very little that you can, or should, try to do about this. We are all born different shapes and sizes after all.

Sadly there is a lot of pressure to become a 'fashionable' shape. If you are in any doubt as to what this is, go and have a look at the magazines on display at the local newsagent. Between all the slimming magazines will be cover after cover showing pretty and thin young women. Although the pressure is less intense on boys, whole generations have been brain-washed to equate beauty with a slim body.

Things will change. Take a look at the pictures painted by 16th and 17th century artists, like Rubens, of women considered beautiful at that time. They are plump, curvy and very well-rounded indeed. In a way these paintings were the equivalent of the fashion and beauty magazines of today.

That's why this book is about healthy eating and good exercise. It is not about trying to create something that a body is not meant to be.

Crash diets

These diets involve eating very few Calories for a very short time – perhaps a week. They are dangerous if continued longer than planned because the body fails to receive vital substances such as vitamins.

In the long term these sorts of diet fail, because you quickly put the 'lost' weight back on when the diet stops.

In addition teenagers have a relatively high energy need. Thus the aim must be for a healthy diet and not just a simple low Calorie one.

Wacky diets

These are always popping up in magazines, books, and newspapers. You might be encouraged to eat one type of fruit, for example, and they are often linked to the name of a famous person who is said to have had a great deal of success with the method.

If they work they do so only by reducing Calorie intake.

Vegetarian diet

Vegetarian diets are perfectly healthy, especially if the vegetarian is prepared to eat eggs and drink milk.

Vegetarians are often eating the healthiest of diets. They tend to eat plenty of fresh fruit and vegetables, and to avoid sugars and fats. They obviously do not take any animal fats.

These are the alternative sources of protein, vitamins and minerals in a vegetarian diet: milk, eggs and cheese, cereals, nuts and pulses.

DIY healthy eating

Now for some practical things to do. Here are six healthy recipes which you can have fun preparing, and which are delicious to eat. Each of them displays a different aspect of healthy eating. Try them at home and with friends. None of them need complicated ingredients and they're all easy to prepare.

BLUE PROTEIN DIP

60g Danish Blue cheese
120ml natural yogurt
1 finely chopped onion
A few drops of lemon juice

Mix all the ingredients together in a bowl and chill in the fridge. Serve with fresh sliced vegetables. Choose from carrots, celery, peppers, mushrooms and cauliflower.

Health tip
This vegetarian dip is high in protein although it contains no meat.

VEGETARIAN SOUP (SERVES TWO)

500g fresh vegetables – a mixture taken from the following: carrots, onions, tomatoes, potatoes, celery, leeks and courgettes
500ml vegetable stock
500ml semi-skimmed milk
1 bay leaf
Salt and pepper

Grate the vegetables on a coarse grater. Place in a saucepan with the stock, milk, bay leaf and seasoning. Cover and bring to the boil. Simmer for not more than 20 minutes.

Health tip

Fresh vegetables have more vitamins than those stored. Keep them in a fridge if necessary, as this will maintain freshness. Chop the vegetables just before cooking. This reduces oxidation in air and resulting vitamin loss. Cut or grate into large pieces, so that fewer nutrients are washed out in cooking.

BAKED JACKET POTATO

1 medium-sized potato
1 portion of baked beans

Bake potato in an oven for 1 hour. Heat up a portion of baked beans in a saucepan towards the end of the potato's cooking hour. Remove potato from the oven and cut in half. Pour beans over cut halves of the potato.

Health tip

This recipe is high in fibre. Although the fibre in the potato and beans is not actually digested, it makes for a healthy passage of food through the intestines.

SARDINES ON TOAST

120g sardines (1 tin in brine, drained)
Juice from ½ lemon
1 chopped tomato
1 chopped spring onion
4 slices of wholemeal bread
75g grated Cheddar or Edam cheese
Ground black pepper

Mash up the sardines with the pepper and lemon juice. Mix in the tomato and onion. Toast one side of the bread, then spread the sardine mixture on the untoasted side. Sprinkle grated cheese on top and toast until the cheese goes brown and bubbly.

Health tip

Fish is a high protein food. Oily fish like sardines contain unsaturated fats which can help prevent heart disease. Pepper and lemon give flavour rather than added salt.

STEAK STEW (SERVES TWO)

350g stewing steak
1 tablespoon plain flour
½ teaspoon dried thyme
1 medium onion (chopped)
1 sliced carrot
1 stick of celery (chopped)
250ml water
1 tablespoon tomato purée
Black pepper

Cube the meat and mix with the flour in a casserole dish. Add remaining ingredients. Cover and cook in a pre-heated oven at 150°C for at least 2 hours. Serve with jacket potato and green vegetables.

Health tip

This way of cooking the meat dramatically reduces the fat content, in comparison to fried steak.

RUNNY HONEY FRUIT SLICES

1 banana
100g pineapple chunks
4 teaspoons of natural yoghurt
2 teaspoons of runny honey
A pinch of ground cinnamon

Peel banana and cut into slices. Arrange the fruit on a plate. Mix the honey, yogurt and cinnamon. Spread the mixture over the fruit. Garnish with grated lemon or orange peel.

Health tip

Honey and banana contain energy. Use fresh pineapple, if possible, rather than chunks from a tin.

Food, health and travel

It is often hard to believe when you are staying in a hotel in a country's capital that the tap water is unsafe to clean your teeth in. It can be true, however. I've travelled with someone who became very ill from doing just this. We take our 'Western' public health service very much for granted.

Not all of the following tips will be relevant to every foreign holiday, but many will be. Take your travel agent's advice on hotels, and especially beware when travelling 'rough', *au natural*, or 'going local'.

Healthy travellers tips

Top ten ways to avoid illness from food in countries where public health standards are poor:

1. Be careful of eating shellfish, especially if you don't know what the creatures were feeding on when caught.
2. Peel fruit before eating. Thick skinned fruit such as bananas are safer than thin skinned tomatoes. Avoid salad plants such as lettuce, which may have been washed in contaminated water.
3. Eat only well-cooked fish and meats.
4. Drink only boiled water. If boiling it yourself, boil for 5 minutes and add another minute for every 1000 feet you are above 5000 feet.
5. Beware of local milk which should be boiled before use. Campers can easily carry powdered milk from home.
6. Avoid uncooked vegetables.
7. Avoid 'local' ice cream, buy only from reputable firms.
8. When eating out drink bottled water, and ensure the cap has not been tampered with. Some places simply re-use empty mineral water bottles and fill them up from the tap!
9. If you buy food, say a samosa, from a roadside stall watch it being cooked.
10. Avoid ice in drinks.

CHAPTER 14

Vitamins

Vitamins are substances which, although only present in food in minute amounts, are vital for life. The 'vita' part of their name comes from the Latin word for 'life'. Vitamins enable the body to function properly, and they need to be eaten since the body cannot make them in sufficient quantities. A good mixed diet will contain all the vitamins you need.

There are about twenty vitamins, and the most important ones are listed in the vitamin chart which follows. You can see in which foods they occur and what they do. As each vitamin was discovered it was given a letter of the alphabet as a name. Later when the exact chemical structure was identified proper names were given. However, many of the vitamins are still known by their letter of the alphabet.

In the past some diseases caused by a lack of vitamins were very common. In the 15th and 16th centuries scurvy (lack of Vitamin C) caused more deaths among European sailors than wars, pirates and shipwrecks put together. This was because on long voyages the sailors went without fresh fruit – an excellent source of Vitamin C. The scurvy that resulted caused their teeth to fall out and their gums to bleed; many died.

However, some vitamins are dangerous in excess. Vitamin A, for example, can be a poison. Polar bear and husky dog liver is very rich in Vitamin A, and somehow Eskimos and husky dogs know this and avoid eating it. In 1912 two hungry Antarctic explorers short of food ate the livers of their husky dogs. One died and the other found his skin peeled off.

Food file

Nutritionists and other food specialists group various foods together as a convenient way of referring to food types in general. These are the 'groups' used in our *Vitamin Chart*.

Pulses: peas, beans, lentils.

Green (leafy) vegetables: cabbage, lettuce, spinach, and broccoli.

Cereals: edible grains of crops such as wheat, maize, barley and rice. Wheat is usually ground into flour before being used to make food such as bread. The 'whole grain' refers to the outer layer of the grains being left when the grain is milled. The outer layer is a good source of fibre and some vitamins. Usually the centre of the grain is used with a variable amount of these outer layers. The outer layers are sometimes called bran.

Oily fish: mackerel, sardines, herring, salmon, pilchards, and sprats.

Yeast extract: foods like Marmite

Citrus fruits: oranges, lemons, and limes.

Dairy products: cheese, milk, butter, and yoghurt.

Vegetable oils: oil from plants such as soya beans, sunflower seeds, and palms.

Vitamin chart

Vitamin	Food sources	Action
Vitamin A (retinol)	Liver, kidney, carrots, dark green vegetables, eggs, milk, butter, margarine, cheese, and oily fish such as salmon, herrings, and mackerel.	Aids growth of body cells, and helps to maintain healthy teeth and bones. Keeps skin healthy. Also helps night vision.
Thiamin (Vitamin B1)	All animal and plant tissues contain thiamin. Rich sources are: cereal grains, nuts, peas, beans, and yeast extract. Flesh foods with a good thiamin source are: fish, pork, and liver.	With other vitamins, thiamin is involved in growth, carbohydrate breakdown, and maintaining the nervous system.

Vitamin	Food sources	Action
Riboflavin (Vitamin B2)	Liver, milk, cheese, eggs, beef, whole cereals, yeast extract, green leafy vegetables, dairy foods, nuts, vegetables, meat, soya and yeast products.	Essential for growth and general health. Helps to maintain healthy hair and tissue. Assists in digestion.
Nicotinic acid or niacin	Meat, whole grains, cheese, eggs, fish, nuts, yeast, and some vegetables, like potatoes and peas.	Needed for growth. Aids digestion and helps to maintain healthy skin and nervous system.
Pantothenic acid	Meat, cereal products, nuts, eggs and vegetables.	Aids growth and maintenance of healthy tissue. Helps production of nerve chemicals and the release of energy from fat.
Pyridoxine (Vitamin B6)	Meat, fish, poultry, green vegetables, yeast, milk, cereal products.	Helps in the making of hormones, enzymes and chemicals. Is involved in the working of nerves. General maintenance of healthy tissue.
Vitamin B12 (cyanocobalamin)	Meat (especially liver), egg yolk, dairy products such as cheese and milk. Fish and yeast extract. (B12 is the only vitamin *not* found in plants. Most vegetarians drink milk and get an adequate supply.)	Essential for red blood cell formation, and all other tissues where new cells are being formed. Helps maintain a healthy skin and nervous tissue.
Folic Acid	Meat (especially liver), green vegetables (especially broccoli tops), pulses, bread, oranges, bananas.	Works with Vitamin B12 to keep blood healthy. Also needed for growth and to maintain the nervous system.

Vitamin	Food sources	Action
Biotin	Liver and other offal, egg yolk, fresh vegetables, and nuts.	Involved in releasing energy from food. Needed for healthy skin and blood vessels.
Vitamin C (ascorbic acid)	Citrus fruits, green vegetables, tomatoes and potatoes.	Wound healing, maintaining healthy skin, bones, teeth and blood vessels. Helps resist infection.
Vitamin D (calciferol)	Only a few foods provide this vitamin. Rich sources are the liver oils of fish, like cod liver oil, and oily fish. Also butter, margarine, and eggs.	Regulates body calcium and with this healthy formation of bone and teeth.
Vitamin E (tocopherols)	Vegetable oils are a rich source. Nuts, leafy green vegetables, margarine. Widely found throughout the human diet.	Not completely understood yet. Rats fed very low Vitamin E diets had a poor sex life (see below).
Vitamin K (phylioquinone)	Vegetables such as cabbage, cauliflower, spinach and sprouts are good sources. Few other foods apart from liver contain much Vitamin K. (About half the body's Vitamin K needs are made by bacteria in the intestines.)	Vitamin K is responsible for certain blood clotting factors in the body.

If you are eating a well-balanced diet, and are fit and well it will be almost impossible for you to become vitamin deficient. It follows on from this that it will not be necessary to buy vitamin supplements.

Some vitamins are so widely found in human food that deficiencies are unknown in normal life. In experiments in California in 1923 rats fed a low Vitamin E diet failed to reproduce. Male rats became sterile and the females failed to become pregnant even with normal males. Vitamin E is so widely spread in human foods that a healthy person on a natural diet has never become deficient in the vitamin like these unfortunate rats. However, what happened to the sex life of these American rodents in 1923 would seem to make a powerful case for eating a normal diet.

CHAPTER 15

Essential Minerals

The human body is made up of a number of elements. These include hydrogen, oxygen, carbon, sodium, potassium, calcium, sulphur, chlorine (as chloride) iron and zinc. All these are essential and are present in quite large amounts. For example an adult human body contains four grams of iron and two grams of zinc.

There are also a number of 'trace elements' or minerals, which the body needs, but which are only present in very small amounts. Until recently it was impossible, or very difficult, to identify many of the body minerals because they are only present in such tiny amounts.

In total your body needs about twenty different minerals. These micronutrients are so widespread in foods, that with two exceptions, you are very unlikely to run short if you eat a varied diet. In addition it is impossible to change or destroy them by cooking.

The two exceptions are:
- Iron during pregnancy, when a mother-to-be may need to take extra iron.
- Fluoride which, when present in sufficient quantities, can prevent tooth decay. There are low-fluoride areas in the United Kingdom, and if you live in one of them, it may be advisable to use fluoride toothpaste, or even to take extra fluoride in the diet. It is worth asking your dentist about this.

Many of these minerals are involved in body cell chemical reactions which produce energy from food. These reactions are actively promoted by enzyme systems which rely on these minerals.

In addition minerals such as sodium (as sodium chloride, or salt) keep a vital chemical balance within body cells.

Essential body minerals:

Calcium
Needed for bones and teeth, and for blood clotting. Also involved in muscle activity and nerve impulse transmission.
   Sources: dairy foods, sardines, and eggs.

Copper
Part of many of the body's enzyme systems. Needed with iron to make the haemoglobin of red blood cells.
   Sources: meat, shell fish, and green vegetables.

Fluoride
Essential for healthy teeth.
   Sources: water and toothpaste.

Iodine
Used by the thyroid gland to make the hormone concerned with body metabolism.
   Sources: sea food. Iodine is often added to table salt.

Iron
Needed to make the haemoglobin of the blood's red cells. This substance enables the red cells to carry oxygen around the body.
   Sources: meat — especially liver and kidney, cocoa, and dried apricots.

Magnesium
Concerned with the release of energy within body cells. Also needed for muscle and nerve activity.
   Sources: widespread in food. Most vegetables as it is a component of chlorophyll. Milk eggs, meat.

Manganese
Involved with several body enzyme systems.
   Sources: tea, coffee, cereals, pulses, and leafy vegetables.

Phosphorus
With calcium forms most of the hard structure of bones and teeth. All body cells need it to store energy.
   Sources: present in all natural or unprocessed foods.

Potassium
Similar to sodium.
   Sources: present in most foods.

Sodium
Concerned with the maintenance of body fluids.
   Sources: present in most foods. Often added to foods as sodium chloride — 'salt'.

Sulphur
Involved in several enzyme systems.
   Sources: meat, fish, eggs, and cereals.

Zinc
Present in many enzymes.
   Sources: meat, seafood and pulses, wholegrain cereals.

Of these essential body minerals, many

of which are present in only minute amounts, two of the most abundant and important are iron and calcium.

Iron

Most foods contain some iron, and it is rarely necessary for teenagers to take extra. As young people grow their need for iron increases, because of their increasing volume of blood.

A fourteen-year-old person needs about 12 milligrams of iron each day. You are likely to get your iron from a mixture of foods rather than from 100 milligrams of treacle.

Iron is the body mineral that you are most likely to run short of, so here is a check list of foods with high levels of iron.

Top Ten foods with iron (mg of iron per 100g of food)

1. Black (blood) sausage   20.0mg
2. Raw green leafy vegetables   18.0mg
3. Liver   14.0mg
4. Pulses   14.0mg
5. Treacle   11.3mg
6. Dried fruit   10.6mg
7. Plain chocolate   4.4mg
8. Raw fresh beef   4.3mg
9. Whole fresh eggs   3.0mg
10. Potatoes (root vegetables) 2.0mg

Calcium

Ninety-nine per cent of the body calcium is in the bones. The other very important one per cent is involved with blood clotting and the correct working of the nervous system. Aged fourteen, you need just under one gram of calcium per day. This is the amount in three glasses of milk or a lump of hard cheese the size of a snooker ball. However, like all other minerals you can get your daily needs from a selection of food.

Appendix

Food composition

In 100 grams these foods average the following:

Food	Energy (in Cals)	Protein (in gms)	Fat (in gms)	Carbohydrate (in gms)
All-Bran	275	13.5	5.1	55
Almonds	580	18.5	53.5	4.3
Apples:				
eating	46	0.3	Nil	12
cooking (baked)	38	0.3	Nil	9.8
Apple pie	190	1.9	7.5	30
Apricots:				
dried	183	4.8	Nil	43.4
fresh	28	0.6	Nil	6.7
tinned in syrup	106	0.5	Nil	27.7
Asparagus (boiled)	18	3.4	Nil	1.1
Bacon:				
lean grilled	290	30.5	18.9	Nil
streaky fried	496	23	44.8	Nil
Banana	77	1.1	Nil	19.2

Food	Energy (in Cals)	Protein (in gms)	Fat (in gms)	Carbohydrate (in gms)
Beans:				
baked	64	5.1	0.5	10.3
broad	48	4	0.5	7
butter	27.3	19.1	1.1	50
kidney	272	22.2	1.7	45
runner	19	1.8	1.9	Nil
Beansprouts	9	1.6	Nil	0.8
Beef:				
beefburger	264	20.4	17.3	7
corned	217	27	12	Nil
grilled rump	168	28.6	6	Nil
sirloin roast, fat and meat	285	23.7	21.1	Nil
meat only	192	27.6	9	Nil
Beer:				
draught bitter	32	0.3	Nil	2.3
bottled lager	29	0.2	Nil	1.5
pale ale bottled	32	0.3	Nil	2
Beetroot (boiled)	44	1.8	Nil	9.9
Biscuits:				
cream crackers	443	9.6	16.3	68.3
digestive	475	9.8	20.5	65
plain	435	7	13.2	75.3
ginger	447	5.9	16.7	71.2
sweet	556	5.5	30.7	66.5
Blackberries (raw)	29	1.3	Nil	6.4
Black currants	59	0.8	Nil	15
Brazil nuts	631	12.9	61.5	4.1
Bread:				
white	234	8	1.5	50
toasted	299	9.6	1.7	64.9
wholemeal	216	9	3	42
brown	224	9	2	45
Broccoli (boiled)	16	3.1	Nil	1
Brussels sprouts (boiled)	17	2.6	Nil	1.7
Butter	741	0.4	50	Nil

FOOD COMPOSITION

Food	Energy (in Cals)	Protein (in gms)	Fat (in gms)	Carbohydrate (in gms)
Cabbage:				
red (raw)	20	1.7	Nil	3.5
spring (boiled)	7	1.1	Nil	0.8
white (raw)	22	1.9	Nil	3.8
winter (raw)	25	2.2	Nil	3.8
Cake:				
fruit	355	4.7	13.5	58.3
sponge	308	8.9	7	55.1
Carrots:				
boiled and raw	22	0.8	Nil	4.4
tinned	19	0.7	Nil	4.4
Cauliflower (boiled)	10	1.6	Nil	1
Celery (raw)	8	0.9	Nil	1.3
Cheese:				
Camembert	304	2.8	23	Nil
cottage	95	13.5	4	1.5
Cheddar	405	26	34	Nil
cream	440	3	48	Nil
Danish blue	360	23	29.2	Nil
Edam	308	24.4	22.9	Nil
processed	350	22.5	28.3	Nil
Stilton	473.5	25.6	40	Nil
Wensleydale	406	29.3	30.7	Nil
Cherries (eating)	47	0.6	Nil	11.9
Chestnuts	171	2.2	2.7	36.6
Chocolate:				
drinking	366	5.5	6	77
milk	559	8.5	33.8	56.7
plain	535	5.1	32.2	58.5
Chicken (roast)				
meat and skin	216	22.5	14	Nil
meat only	148	24.8	55	Nil
Cider:				
dry	37	Nil	Nil	2.64
sweet	42	Nil	Nil	4.28
Cockles	48	11	0.3	Nil
Cocoa powder	452	20.4	25.6	35

Food	Energy (in Cals)	Protein (in gms)	Fat (in gms)	Carbohydrate (in gms)
Cod:				
fried	140	20	4.7	2.9
grilled	160	27	5.3	Nil
Coffee:				
ground and roasted	301	12.5	15.4	28.5
instant	156	4	0.7	35.5
Cornflakes	368	8.6	1.6	86.5
Crab:				
boiled	127	19.5	5.2	Nil
tinned	81	18	1	Nil
Cream:				
double	456	1.5	48.2	2
single	217	2.4	21.2	3.2
Cucumber	10	0.6	Nil	2
Currants (dried)	243	1.7	Nil	63
Damsons (raw)	38	0.5	Nil	9.6
Dates	248	2	Nil	63.9
Doughnuts	352	6	15.8	48.8
Duck (roast): meat only	189	25.3	29	Nil
Eggs:				
fresh (boiled, raw)	161	12	12	Nil
fried	239	14.1	19.5	Nil
white only	37	9	Nil	Nil
yolk only	350	16.2	30.5	Nil
Figs:				
dried	214	3.6	Nil	52.9
green	41	1.3	Nil	9.5
Fish (paste)	174	14.9	9.5	6.5
Fruit gums	172	1	Nil	45
Fruit salad (tinned in syrup)	94	0.3	Nil	25
Gooseberries (fresh)	37	0.6	Nil	9.2
Goose (roast)	320	28.5	22.4	Nil

FOOD COMPOSITION

Food	Energy (in Cals)	Protein (in gms)	Fat (in gms)	Carbohydrate (in gms)
Grapes:				
black	60	0.6	Nil	15.5
white	63	0.6	Nil	16.1
Grapefruit				
fresh	22	0.6	Nil	5.3
tinned	60	0.6	Nil	5.3
Greengages (stewed with sugar)	75	0.6	Nil	19.2
Haddock:				
steamed	97	22.4	0.8	Nil
fried	175	20.4	8.3	3.6
smoked and steamed	100	22.3	0.9	Nil
Ham:				
boiled lean only	219	23.1	13.4	Nil
boiled lean and fat	435	16.3	39.6	Nil
chopped	340	15.2	29.9	Nil
tinned	120	18.4	5.1	Nil
Hazel nuts	398	9	36	6.8
Heart (sheep roast)	239	25	14.7	Nil
Herring (grilled)	217	211	15	0.75
Honey (in pot)	288	0.4	Nil	76.4
Jam	261	0.6	Nil	69
Jam tarts	394	3.8	15.4	62.7
Jelly:				
made with water	60	1.7	Nil	15
packet	259	6.1	Nil	62.5
Kidney (sheep fried)	170	25	8.5	Nil
Kippers (baked)	201	23.2	11.4	Nil
Lamb:				
chop, grilled	222	27.8	12.3	Nil
leg, roast	191	29.4	8.1	Nil
shoulder, roast	196	23.8	11.2	Nil
Lard	910	Nil	99	Nil
Leeks (boiled)	25	1.8	Nil	4.6
Lemonade	21	Nil	Nil	5.6

Food	Energy (in Cals)	Protein (in gms)	Fat (in gms)	Carbohydrate (in gms)
Lemons	15	0.8	Nil	3.2
Lemon squash	126	0.1	Nil	33.7
Lentils (dry)	295	23.8	Nil	53.2
Lettuce (raw)	11	1.1	Nil	1.8
Lime juice (cordial)	112	0.1	Nil	29.8
Liver:				
calf, fried	260	29	14.2	2.2
ox, fried	284	29.5	15.8	4
Loganberries:				
fresh	17	1.1	Nil	3.4
tinned	101	0.6	Nil	26.2
Lucozade	67	Nil	Nil	17.9
Macaroni (boiled)	114	3.4	0.6	25.2
Mackerel (fried)	187	20.7	11.3	Nil
Mango	59	0.5	Nil	15.2
Margarine:				
hard and soft	730	0.1	82	0.1
low fat spread	365	Nil	41	Nil
polyunsaturated	730	0.1	81	0.1
Marmalade	261	0.1	Nil	69.5
Marmite	6	1.4	Nil	Nil
Marrow	7	0.4	Nil	1.4
Mars Bar	441	5.3	18.9	0.7
Melon:				
cantaloupe	24	1	Nil	5.3
yellow	21	0.6	Nil	5
Milk:				
dried, skimmed	333	35	0.5	55
condensed, tinned	338	8.2	10.5	56
fresh, whole	66	3.4	3.7	4.8
fresh, skimmed	35	3.5	0.2	5.1
tinned, evaporated	158	8.6	9	11.3
Mincemeat (sweet)	129	0.6	3.3	25.5

FOOD COMPOSITION

Food	Energy (in Cals)	Protein (in gms)	Fat (in gms)	Carbohydrate (in gms)
Mullet (red, steamed)	128	21.4	4.3	Nil
Muesli:				
home prepared	295	8	7.2	53
packet	368	12.9	7.5	66.2
Mushrooms:				
raw	10	1.8	0.3	Nil
fried	217	2.2	22.3	Nil
Mussels (boiled)	87	17	2	Nil
Oatmeal porridge	45	1.4	0.9	8.2
Olive oil	930	Nil	99.9	Nil
Onions:				
mature	23	0.9	Nil	5.2
spring	35	0.9	Nil	8.5
fried	355	1.8	33.3	10.1
Oranges	35	0.8	Nil	8.5
Orange (juice)	38	0.6	Nil	9.4
Orange (squash)	120	0.1	Nil	30
Ovaltine	384	13.2	6.3	72.3
Oysters (raw)	50	10.2	0.9	Nil
Pasta:				
raw	118	4.1	0.75	24
tinned in tomato sauce	59	1.7	0.7	12.2
Pastry:				
flakey, baked	589	6.7	42	45.6
short, baked	548	7.7	33.4	54.9
Parsnips (boiled)	56	1.3	Nil	13.5
Peaches:				
fresh	37	0.6	Nil	9.1
tinned in syrup	87	0.4	Nil	22.9
Peanuts	595	27	49	8.6
Pears:				
English, eating	40	0.2	Nil	10.4
tinned in syrup	77	0.4	Nil	20

Food	Energy (in Cals)	Protein (in gms)	Fat (in gms)	Carbohydrate (in gms)
Peas:				
fresh, boiled	49	5	Nil	7.7
tinned, processed	83	6	0.2	13.6
Peppermints	391	0.5	0.7	102.2
Peppers (sweet)	15	0.9	0.4	2.2
Pilchards:				
tinned in tomato sauce	126	18.8	5.4	0.7
Pineapple:				
fresh	46	0.5	Nil	11.6
tinned in syrup	77	0.3	Nil	20.2
Pineapple juice	53	0.4	Nil	13.4
Plaice:				
steamed	92	18.1	1.9	Nil
fried	234	18	14.4	7
Plums				
dessert	38	0.6	Nil	9.6
stewed, no sugar	20	0.4	Nil	4.8
Pork:				
lean chops, grilled	226	32.4	10.6	Nil
lean leg, roasted	185	30.6	7	Nil
Potatoes:				
boiled	80	1.5	0.1	20
baked	106	2.5	0.1	30
mashed	120	1.5	5	18
roast	156	3	5	27
frozen chips	290	3	19	29
crisps	534	6	30	50
Prawns	104	21.2	1.8	Nil
Prunes (stewed, no sugar, no stones)	81	1.2	Nil	20.2
Radish	15	1	Nil	2.8
Raisins (dried)	247	1.1	Nil	64.4
Raspberries	25	0.9	Nil	5.6
Red currants (stewed, no sugar)	16	0.8	Nil	3.4
Rhubarb (stewed, no sugar)	5	0.4	Nil	0.8
Ribena	229	0.2	Nil	60.9

FOOD COMPOSITION

Food	Energy (in Cals)	Protein (in gms)	Fat (in gms)	Carbohydrate (in gms)
Rice Krispies	351	5.8	0.7	82.1
Rice:				
brown	120	2.7	0.5	26
pudding	144	3.6	7.6	15.7
white	122	2.1	0.3	29.6
Salmon:				
fresh and steamed	199	19.1	13	Nil
tinned	145	20	8	Nil
Sardines (tinned):				
in oil	217	23.7	13.6	Nil
in sauce	177	17.8	11.6	0.5
Sausage:				
beef, fried	287	13	18	15.2
pork, fried	326	11.5	24.8	12.7
pork, grilled	318	13.3	24.6	11.5
Scampi (fried)	316	12.2	17.6	29
Scones	370	7.5	13.9	56.6
Shortbread	521	6.1	27.2	64.9
Shredded Wheat	362	9.7	2.8	79
Shrimps	114	22.3	2.4	Nil
Skate (fried)	242	15	16.4	7.5
Special K	355	15.3	0.4	78.2
Soya beans	155	13.1	6.8	9
Soup:				
packet	20	0.8	0.3	3.6
tinned, cream	58	1.7	3.8	4.4
Spirits (70% proof)	222	Nil	Nil	Nil
Spinach (boiled)	28	5.1	Nil	1.4
Sprats (fried)	444	22.3	37.9	Nil
Spring greens (boiled)	10	1.7	Nil	0.9
Strawberries	26	0.6	Nil	6.2
Suet	826	Nil	86.6	12

Food	Energy (in Cals)	Protein (in gms)	Fat (in gms)	Carbohydrate (in gms)
Sugar:				
Demerara	394	0.5	Nil	99.5
white	394	Nil	Nil	99.5
Sultanas (dried)	249	1.7	Nil	64.7
Swede (boiled)	18	0.9	Nil	3.8
Sweetcorn:				
boiled	123	4.1	2.3	22.8
tinned	76	2.9	0.5	161
Sweets (boiled)	327	Nil	Nil	87.3
Syrup (golden)	297	0.3	Nil	79
Tangerines	34	0.9	Nil	8
Tea	58	14.1	Nil	Nil
Toffees	432.5	2.1	17.2	71.1
Tomatoes:				
raw	14	1	Nil	3
fried	71	1	5.9	3.3
Tongue	290	18.5	24	Nil
Trifle	150	3.3	5.6	22.4
Tripe (stewed)	102	18	3	Nil
Trout (steamed)	133	22.3	4.5	Nil
Tuna (tinned)	289	22.8	22	Nil
Turkey	80	30.2	7.7	Nil
Turnips (boiled)	11	0.7	Nil	2.3
Walnuts	545	11.75	51.5	5
Watercress (raw)	15	2.9	Nil	0.7
Weetabix	351	10.9	1.9	77
Whitebait (fried)	537	18.5	47.5	5.3
Wine:				
port, ruby	152	0.13	Nil	11.4
red	68	19	Nil	25
sherry, dry	114	19	Nil	1.36
sherry, sweet	135	0.31	Nil	6.88

Food	Energy (in Cals)	Protein (in gms)	Fat (in gms)	Carbohydrate (in gms)
white, dry	66	0.1	Nil	Nil
white, sweet	94	0.2	5.9	Nil
Yoghurt:				
fruit	95	48	1	4.9
low fat	54	4.7	1.8	4.9
natural	52	5	1	6.2
Yorkshire pudding	218	7.1	9.4	27

Strength + Stamina + Suppleness = FITNESS

Suppleness (stretch exercises)	Time: Minutes	Warm-up	Stamina/strength exercises	Warm-down
	1			
	2			
	3			
	4			
	5			
	6			
	7			
	8			
	9			
	10			
	11			
	12			
	13			
	14			
	15			
	16			
	17			
	18			
	19			
	20			

This is the blank template for *your* Personal Fitness Programme, as referred to earlier in the book.